Workbook

Iwonna Dubicka
Lewis Lansford

B2

Business Partner

Contents

1 > Corporate culture

Elements of corporate culture

1 Complete the sentences using the words in the box.

> atmosphere   flexibility   hierarchy   image   open-plan
> organisational   strategy   structure   values

1 Company _____ refers to the way a business is organised.

2 Company _____ is planning a series of actions in order to achieve something.

3 An _____ office is one which does not have walls dividing it into separate rooms.

4 A good _____ in a company means a positive feeling that a place gives employees.

5 The _____ of a company refers to the general opinion that people have of an organisation or product. This is not limited to advertising.

6 Having _____ means being able to change or adapt to a situation.

7 Company _____ means staff are organised on various levels, depending on responsibility, e.g. junior and senior managers.

8 Company _____ are the principles and practices that a business feels are important, e.g. equal pay for men and women, or the way employees are treated.

9 _____ behaviour looks at how people work together and how ways of working, e.g. employee interaction and leadership style, can affect the whole organisation.

2 Read the conversation between an HR manager (HR) and a new intern (I). Choose the correct option.

HR: Do you have any questions for me, Rebecca?

I: Yes, I'd like to know what the working environment is like.

HR: You'll find there's a good [1] *flexibility / company structure / atmosphere* because our staff are friendly and positive. And the [2] *pay rate / dress code / company image* is quite relaxed. It's business casual.

I: And what are the working hours? Are they 9 a.m. to 5 p.m.?

HR: That's right, although we expect employees to have some [3] *flexibility / company values / minimum salaries* and adapt when plans change, for instance, your boss may ask you to work late one day to finish an important task.

I: And does everyone work in a(n) [4] *scaled / incredible / open-plan* area?

HR: Yes. None of the managers has their own office anymore.

I: So what would my monthly pay be?

HR: As you are new to the company, you would be earning the standard [5] *pay structure / minimum salary / open-plan* for interns, which is about €800 a month.

I: €800? Erm … I was hoping for something a little higher.

HR: Well, we could discuss a slightly higher [6] *pay rate / company structure / pay structure* after the six-month trial period.

Grammar Future Continuous and Future Perfect Simple

1 Look at the verb tenses in the example sentences. Which of the tenses describes an activity that ...
   i will be in progress at a particular moment in the future?
   ii will be finished by a certain time in the future?

a *Many young people **will have decided** what is important for them in a job by the time they go to their first interview.*

b *Millennials **will be looking** for jobs with more chances of promotion and more diverse work when they enter the workforce.*

2 Complete the sentences using the tense structures in the box. Then decide which activity will be in progress and which will be finished.

will have transferred   will be retaining   won't have changed   will be staying
Will you be sleeping   will be preparing   Will you have finished   will be entertaining

1 I won't be able to do lunch on Monday as I _____ clients all day.

2 He doesn't need a hotel room for the conference next month as he _____ with his brother.

3 _____ the proposal by the end of the week?

4 The manager won't be taking any calls in the morning as she _____ her presentation.

5 _____ when my flight gets in?

6 Investment banks _____ the way they do business by the end of the next decade. It will take much longer.

7 Our boss said that by the end of the year, our bank _____ its operations to the Warsaw office.

8 The banking sector _____ employees by offering job security rather than high salaries over the next few years.

In progress: ____ ____ ____ ____ ____   **Finished:** ____ ____ ____

3 Complete the conversation with the Future Continuous or Future Perfect Simple form of the verbs in brackets.

A: What kind of job do you think you ¹_____ (do) five years from now?

B: I think I ²_____ (run) my own business.

A: Wow! So you ³_____ (set up) your own company by the time you're twenty-five!

B: Yes, I hope so. We ⁴_____ (finish) our degree course by then, won't we? What about you?

A: I'm not sure. Perhaps I ⁵_____ (work) in investment banking. And what ⁶_____ (you / do) in your free time? I imagine you won't have much time off as an entrepreneur.

B: That's right. I guess I'll be very busy some weekends. But I believe in a good work–life balance, so I hope I ⁷_____ (not / give up) all my interests by my mid-20s. I mean, I ⁸_____ (still go) to the gym, and I think I ⁹_____ (travel) more because I ¹⁰_____ (earn) a good salary. And you? Do you think ¹¹_____ (you / still live) with your parents in the same town?

A: Oh no! I'm sure I ¹²_____ (move out) of my parents' home before then. And maybe I ¹³_____ (live) in a city like Frankfurt or Warsaw.

B: Me too. But I think in five years' time, I ¹⁴_____ (work) somewhere in Asia, perhaps Kuala Lumpur.

Listening

1 🔊 1.01   Listen to an expert talking about employee retention and match the sentence halves. Two of the options (a–f) are <u>not</u> used.

1 The pay rate is important but it isn't ____

2 Little things can make a difference and help to ____

3 Most people want to work for a company where ____

4 Any successful organisation needs a structure ____

a create a good working environment.

b they share the same open-plan office as their colleagues.

c where there are opportunities for promotion and personal development.

d they share the same values as their colleagues.

e every company that offers every Friday afternoon off.

f the only motivational factor that concerns millennials.

2 **Choose the correct option to complete what the expert says. Then listen again to check your answers.**

1 The ____ of employees is something that has been given more importance in recent years.

    a principles   **b** flexibility   **c** behaviour   **d** happiness

2 Millennials often prefer a more ____ dress code compared to their older colleagues.

    a casual   **b** smart-casual   **c** business casual   **d** business-like

3 Those with young children will appreciate having ____ in their work schedule.

    a work–life balance   **b** hierarchy   **c** flexibility   **d** work at home

4 I'd say a company's ____ and beliefs are a decisive factor when accepting a job offer.

    a principles   **b** values   **c** behaviour   **d** atmosphere

5 Asking employees what they think when developing company ____ can make all employees feel more valued and motivated.

    a security   **b** development   **c** strategy   **d** hierarchy

6 This type of motivation helps to ____ staff and encourages growth.

    a develop   **b** train   **c** motivate   **d** retain

3 **Read the sentences summarising the interview and decide if they are *true* (T) or *false* (F).**

1 There are many motivational factors that affect a young person's choice of company. These may include dress code and small things in the working environment. ____

2 The important factors for young people, when they are choosing which company to work for, include opportunities for progression, a large salary, strong management and the company's principles. ____

Functional language

Building trust

1 ◀) 1.02 Complete the conversation between Dominique (Project Manager) and Karl (IT Engineer) using the phrases in the box. Then listen and check your answers. One phrase is <u>not</u> used.

> Could we help you   we both want to   Can I suggest that   how do you think we can
> I can see you're concerned   let's wait until   One way to solve this is
> To be honest, I feel   I understand what you're saying   Would it be useful

D: As I mentioned in our last call, Karl, I think quality is becoming a concern on this project. ¹_____ a little worried about delivering a quality product to the customer.

K: Really? ²_____ about quality, but I thought you were happy that we had managed to reduce costs.

D: Yes, ³_____ keep to budget, but frankly I'm concerned that we're losing quality and our customers won't buy the software. ⁴_____ to test quality more effectively in some way?

K: Well, until now, we've only tested the software using a small number of people. ⁵_____ to test it using another group with very different needs, but we don't have a budget for that.

D: I like your suggestion, Karl, and I realise testing is expensive. Based on your experience, ⁶_____ test the software without increasing the budget too much? Could we reduce the number of testers in the first group, and then create a second group for testing?

K: ⁷_____ but it's important to have at least twelve people in each group and currently we have one group of eighteen testers.

D: ⁸_____ for us to create another group of twelve testers, but reduce the first group from eighteen to twelve? That would mean paying for only six more testers.

K: Sure. That could work. But ⁹_____ we have the test results from this week and then decide together. And we need to make sure the second group have different software requirements.

D: Thanks, Karl. I knew we could come up with something.

Self-presentation

2 ◀) 1.03 Complete the personal presentation with suitable words. The last letter of the words has been given. Then listen and check your answers.

Hello. My name's Lotte Smit and I'm ¹__ __ __ __d in the Tokyo office. I've been with this company for around two years. We work on engineering projects. I'm a Key Account Manager. In the past I ²__ __ __d __o work in Europe, but since last year I've been working on projects in South-East Asia as I'm now ³__ __ __ __ __ __ __ __ __ __ __e __ __r key accounts in Japan and Australia. What else? Well, I have to travel quite a lot; half of my time is spent travelling around Japan, Australia and New Zealand. The job is ⁴__ __ __ __e stressful but I really enjoy it. And I have to say, it's going to be ⁵__ __ __ __t working ⁶__ __ __h you ⁷__n this project and I'm ⁸__ __ __ __d __o be ⁹__ __ __ __ __ __ __d. Finally, if you ¹⁰__ __ __d my help in any ¹¹__ __y, don't ¹²__ __ __ __ __ __ __e to ask. I'm here to collaborate. Thank you.

Writing   A company news blog

1A   Read the blog on the latest news at your organisation and label the paragraphs 1–7 using the headings in the box. You can use some headings more than once.

> Concluding   Introducing   Title   Informing

URGENT: Please revise this text!

STOP PRESS: opportunity to study abroad for one month!

Why not take advantage ~of~ our new study abroad programme? The company happy to announce that it is offering you a free one-month study programme in a country of your choice.

We are offering you the opportunity study in a variety of destinations: Buenos Aires, Munich, Wroclaw, Toronto or Seoul.

There is a variety of courses on offer, including language programmes and introductory MBA programmes so you sure to find something of interest. The courses are on offer at different times during the year and your accommodation will be paid for by the company.

Please note that participants will need to pay an enrolment* fee but this will reimbursed** when you have completed the programme.

Let us know if you wish to participate in this international study programme. Although it is exciting news, we appreciate you likely to have some concerns about going abroad or your choice of country. The HR department can address any concerns you may have by answering your questions.

Please do not hesitate contact us for more information.

*enrolment (noun): the process of arranging to do a course
**reimburse (verb, formal): pay money back to someone

1 _____

2 _____

3 _____

4 _____

5 _____

6 _____

7 _____

B   Read the blog in exercise 1A and correct the language mistakes. There is one error in each section 2-7.

2   Write a blog for your company website with news about an opportunity to work abroad for three months. Write 160–180 words. Use:

- the expressions in bold from Exercise 1A.

- the functional language in Exercise 2 on page 16 in the coursebook.

Include the following:

- **Title:** add an interesting title.

- **Introduction:** introduce the news to the readers.

- **Information:** give more information about the news: think about answers to questions starting with *what, when, where, why* or *how*?

- **Conclusion:** ask the readers to do something, e.g. to send an email, to click on a link.

3   Choose the best option for concluding your blog in Exercise 2. Review your conclusion if necessary.

a   Please don't hesitate to contact us for more information.

b   If you're interested, just click here.

c   Don't hesitate to contact us or click on the link below to find out more about this exciting programme.

Vocabulary Training and development

1 Complete the conversation between two colleagues in the HR department with suitable words. The last two letters of the words have been given.

A: The director is interviewing candidates for some new management positions.

B: I know. We'll need to organise an [1]__ _ _ _ _ _ _on _ _ _ _ _ _ _me for when they start.

A: Yes. And that reminds me, there are a few [2]__ _ _ _ _es interested in doing mentorship programmes.

B: I'm not sure if we have enough mentors this year – everyone is very busy. They might need to do [3]__ _ _ _ _ne _ _ _ _ _ _es instead, or perhaps a combination of face-to-face and online training.

A: That's right. A [4]__ _ _ _ _ _ed _ _ _ _ _ _ _ng programme might be the best delivery method, with a mix of specific [5]__ __b-_ _ _ _ _ed training, depending on the department, combined with skills courses for long-term [6]__ _ _ _ _er _ _ _ _ _ _ _ _ _nt.

B: Sounds good. Let's see how many of these skills courses we can do in-house.

2 Complete the table with the correct word forms.

Noun(s)	Verb	Adjective
analysis	analyse	[1]_____
[2]_____	–	competent
development	*develop*	*developed* / *developing*
[3]_____	–	intelligent
[4]_____ (*person*) / learning (*process*)	learn	learned / learning
mentor (*person*) / [5]_____ (*person*) / [6]_____ (*process*)	mentor	–
[7]_____	motivate	[8]_____ / motivating
[9]_____ (*person*) / trainee (*person*) / training (*process*)	[10]_____	trained

3 A training and development expert is describing different kinds of training. Complete her blog using the words and phrases in the box.

> benchmarking emotional learning needs analysis
> training courses skills set standard understanding

Why learn?

Motivation is an essential part of learning. Without it, we wouldn't learn anything.

When we design training or development programmes, we generally begin with a [1]_____. This is because we have to know what level of [2]_____ employees already have of a particular job or skill.

In Human Resources, we often talk about people's competencies, which are the specific skills they need to do a particular job. In order for these to keep developing, an organisation should offer staff practical [3]_____ that are job- or task-oriented with short-term goals. However, long-term development programmes should develop a wider [4]_____, such as communication skills and [5]_____ intelligence. Companies nowadays use a combination of these types of programmes.

It's also very important for the HR department of an organisation to be able to evaluate how effective the training is. One way of doing this is [6]_____, which is using a company's good performance as a [7]_____ by which to judge the performance of other companies of the same type or in the same sector.

Finally, I completely agree with the saying, 'We never stop [8]_____.' Training and development are essential if we are to continue to grow and develop as human beings.

Grammar   Modals in the passive voice

1 Change the sentences from the active to the passive form. Use the modal verb that is <u>underlined</u>.

1 HR <u>should</u> train all staff how to use the blended learning platform.
All staff _____ how to use the blended learning platform.

2 HR <u>needs to</u> improve the quality of in-house training we offer.
The quality of in-house training courses HR offers _____ .

3 The company <u>must</u> hold language courses for those who work with international clients.
Language courses _____ for those who work with international clients.

4 We <u>can't</u> offer development courses to everyone as we'll go over budget.
Development courses _____ to everyone as we'll go over budget.

5 Those who don't give presentations <u>don't have to</u> do the presentations course.
The presentations course _____ by those who don't give presentations.

6 The trainer <u>shouldn't</u> teach this aspect of communication skills because it was covered on the last course.
This aspect of communication skills _____ because it was covered on the last course.

7 Does the trainer <u>have to</u> give all participants a feedback questionnaire to fill in?
Do all participants _____ a feedback questionnaire to fill in?

8 We <u>have to</u> decide if we <u>should</u> teach this skill to all employees, or just a small number of them.
It _____ if all employees _____ this skill, or just a small number of them.

2 Decide what function the modal verb has in each sentence.

1 In-house training ought to be given by the company's own staff members.

   a permission   **b** recommendation   **c** prohibition   **d** obligation

2 Our department may be moved to another building in the next six months.

   a ability   **b** necessity   **c** prohibition   **d** possibility

3 All desks in the office have to be cleared at the end of each working day.

   a obligation   **b** permission   **c** recommendation **d** possibility

4 More time to complete your project would be considered if you asked for it.

   a permission   **b** possibility   **c** prohibition   **d** obligation

5 The extra costs need to be considered before we make any changes.

   a recommendation **b** possibility   **c** prohibition   **d** necessity

6 Your final report must be submitted by next Friday.

   a recommendation **b** possibility   **c** obligation   **d** ability

Reading **1** Read a training manager's notes on the training and development needs of an organisation providing public transport services. Complete his notes using the course titles in the box.

> Communication skills and conflict resolution   Mindfulness: dealing with stress
> Designing career development programmes   Designing online learning platforms
> Health and safety: training your guard dog   Repairing buses or trains
> Motivating staff: communicating with remote teams   Report writing

Company training and development needs

○ <u>Marketing and communication</u>
Course: improve your presentation skills; participants watch videos at home, record themselves giving a presentation and are then sent personalised feedback from in-house trainers

○ <u>HR department</u> – need for long-term development planning to retain employees
Course: [1]_____ ; face-to-face sessions offered to a select number of employees on the mentorship programme

○ <u>Finance</u> – complaints from other departments that financial reports are badly written
Course: [2]_____ ; to be given online

○ <u>IT department</u> – we're changing our online learning system!
Online course: [3]_____

○ <u>Managers</u> – some employees say they aren't motivated and have little contact with managers
Course: [4]_____ ; part of the blended learning programme for managers

<u>Security staff</u> – job-oriented, practical training required, materials on the Intranet
Course: [5]_____

○ <u>Train drivers</u> – drivers are often very stressed and some are on extended sick leave
Course: [6]_____ ; five workshops focusing on relaxation techniques

<u>Customer service dept.</u> – complaints from angry passengers; all staff need to be trained
Course: [7]_____ ; blended learning with a training manual and simulations

○ <u>Technical maintenance</u> – job-related practical training courses required depending on area
Course: [8]_____ ; hands-on approach including demonstrations

2 Look again at the training manager's notes in Exercise 1. Complete the table using the words in the box.

> **Type of training:** job-oriented   mentorship programme   career development
> **Delivery:** face-to-face   online learning   blended learning

Course	Type of training	Delivery
Communication skills and conflict resolution	*career development*	*blended learning*
Designing career development programmes	*mentorship programme*	[1]_____
Designing online learning platforms	[2]_____	[3]_____
Health and safety: training your guard dog	[4]_____	[5]_____
Mindfulness: dealing with stress	[6]_____	[7]_____
Motivating staff: communicating with remote teams	[8]_____	[9]_____
Repairing buses or trains	[10]_____	[11]_____
Report writing	[12]_____	[13]_____

3 Which course(s) in Exercise 2 would be the most useful for ...

1 a station manager?   **3** a teacher?

2 a public relations employee?   **4** a surveyor?

Functional language

Exchanging ideas

1 **Read the expressions and choose the correct function.**

1 What do you think we should do? / What's the best way to handle this?

    a requesting ideas   **b** responding to ideas   **c** giving ideas

2 One option could be to create more detailed requirements.

    a moving from idea to decision   **b** requesting ideas   **c** giving ideas

3 I don't think it makes sense to look at the requirements again.

    a requesting ideas   **b** developing ideas   **c** responding to ideas

4 Just picking up on what Max just said, why don't we … ? / If I can add to this, I think …

    a moving from idea to decision   **b** developing ideas   **c** requesting ideas

5 Do we all agree with Ksenia's idea? / So, shall we try that?

    a moving from idea to decision   **b** developing ideas   **c** contributing ideas

Facilitating a discussion

2A 🔊 2.01   **Complete the beginning and end of a conference call using the phrases in the box. One phrase is <u>not</u> used. Then listen and check your answers.**

> we have made good progress   I'm afraid time is pressing   so, just to recap
> we can then decide on   it's important for everyone   I want to come to that
> what we're looking to do here today   and then discuss

Extract 1

C: Good morning, everyone. Thank you for joining us on this call. ¹_____ is to choose the best digital learning platform. First we'll hear from Valeria from IT. Then, as we discuss things, ²_____ to contribute their ideas.

T: Hi Carrie, Thom here in Berlin. Can we talk about budget, as I think this has a massive impact on the way we digitalise everything?

C: Oh sorry, Thom, ³_____ later but can we just go around the table first ⁴_____ ? …

Extract 2

C: That's great, Valeria. ⁵_____ everything, we all agree to offer more online courses, and some blended learning, and Thom thinks that the digital platform will definitely reduce trainings costs. I think ⁶_____ here today. Perhaps the next step would be to look at the risks when digitalising learning, especially for certain skills courses that we usually do face-to-face. It is definitely important, but ⁷_____ , so we'll need to discuss this in our next call …

B **How well do you think Carrie does as a facilitator? Listen again to the conference call to check your answer.**

a Carrie does quite well but forgets to summarise what was decided.

b Carrie manages interruptions and technical issues quite well.

c Carrie doesn't do very well because she doesn't contribute much.

Writing   A training request

1A Read the email from a sales manager requesting a training course. Write the correct form of the words in brackets.

To: HR Manager

Re: Request for extended induction training*

Dear Giovanna,

¹I am writing to request extended induction training for new employees. As I have just been made an in-house trainer, I have been asked to organise induction training for new staff next month.

I (belief) new employees need to learn about the services we provide and how the company works, as well as our corporate culture. However, ²staff who are new to the company say they don't receive enough training during the one-day induction course that is offered – please see the (attach) feedback questionnaires.

³I would, therefore, like to organise a three-day intensive induction course ⁴to meet the needs of new staff members and to (motivation) them in their first days of work. ⁵I would (appreciation) it if you could let me know by the end of the week ⁶because we will need to finalise the induction content as soon as (possibility). I attach a suggested induction programme for your information.

Furthermore, ⁷I am (interest) in doing the course in presentation skills so that I can further develop my skills as a trainer. ⁸It would be very (help) as I do not have much experience in this area. ⁹Would it be possible for me to (attendance) this course?

Kind regards
Davood Patil

*induction training: the introduction of someone into a new job, company, or official position

a *believe* _____

b _____

c _____
d _____

e _____

f _____

g _____
h _____

B Look at the underlined phrases (1–9) in the email in Exercise 1A. Which are requests and which are reasons?

Requests: ____ ____ ____ ____   Reasons: ____ ____ ____ ____ ____

2 Write an email applying for a course in designing online learning platforms. Write 160–180 words. Use:

- expressions from the model text in Exercise 1A.
- functional language in Exercises 2A and 2B on page 26 in the coursebook.

Include the following:

- **Name of the course**
- **Where**, e.g. in-house training or an external course
- **Length of the course**, e.g. a five-day course, or thirty hours
- **When**, e.g. include a request for a suitable time
- **How**, e.g. delivery method: face-to-face, online or blended learning
- **Why**, e.g. reason(s) for request(s)

Vocabulary   Finance and economic crises

1 Use the clues to complete the crossword. The first letter of the words has been given.

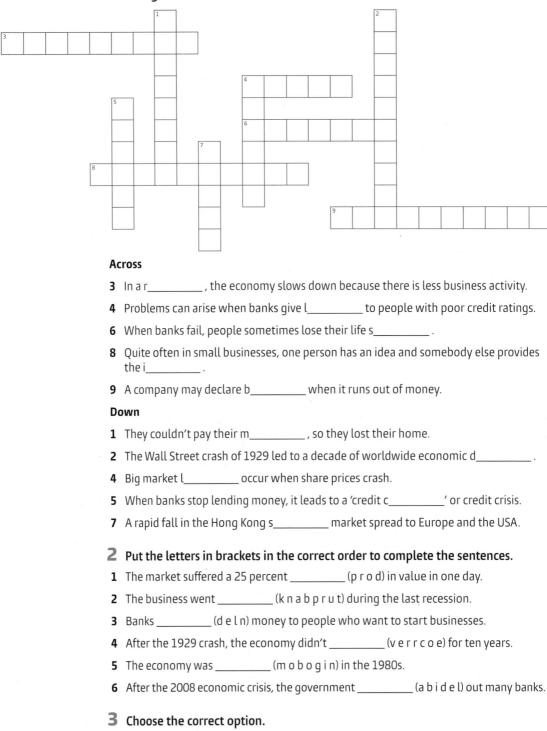

Across

3 In a r_____ , the economy slows down because there is less business activity.

4 Problems can arise when banks give l_____ to people with poor credit ratings.

6 When banks fail, people sometimes lose their life s_____ .

8 Quite often in small businesses, one person has an idea and somebody else provides the i_____ .

9 A company may declare b_____ when it runs out of money.

Down

1 They couldn't pay their m_____ , so they lost their home.

2 The Wall Street crash of 1929 led to a decade of worldwide economic d_____ .

4 Big market l_____ occur when share prices crash.

5 When banks stop lending money, it leads to a 'credit c_____' or credit crisis.

7 A rapid fall in the Hong Kong s_____ market spread to Europe and the USA.

2 Put the letters in brackets in the correct order to complete the sentences.

1 The market suffered a 25 percent _____ (p r o d) in value in one day.

2 The business went _____ (k n a b p r u t) during the last recession.

3 Banks _____ (d e l n) money to people who want to start businesses.

4 After the 1929 crash, the economy didn't _____ (v e r r c o e) for ten years.

5 The economy was _____ (m o b o g i n) in the 1980s.

6 After the 2008 economic crisis, the government _____ (a b i d e l) out many banks.

3 Choose the correct option.

1 There was a major stock market *crash / period* in 1929.

2 It's difficult to buy a house if you have a poor credit *crisis / rating*.

3 A few years ago, there was a global economic *downturn / market* that started in Asia.

4 A serious problem in one market generally affects the entire global *finance / economy*.

5 Financial *productions / institutions* such as banks are responsible for lending money to individuals and businesses.

6 A *devastating / depressing* drop in a market's value is almost always felt in the economy.

Grammar Expressing certainty and probability

1 Complete the sentences using the correct form of the words and phrases in the box.

| be likely to | be unlikely to | be unlikely that | be due to | probably | be likely that |

1 The company has been very profitable, so it _____ it will open more stores.

2 With recent sponsorship deals, they _____ increase their revenue even more.

3 The CEO _____ make an announcement about the company's plans at three o'clock this afternoon.

4 They've recently increased the dividend, so it _____ shareholders will complain.

5 Their brand is incredibly popular, so they _____ have problems getting celebrity endorsement.

6 Profitability will _____ continue to increase as the company grows.

2 Rewrite the sentences using the words in brackets.

1 The marketing strategy is certain to be a success. (definitely)

The marketing strategy _____ .

2 They'll probably open a new store in Tokyo. (probable)

_____ they'll open a new store in Tokyo.

3 They're going to launch a new line next week. (due)

_____ launch a new line next week.

4 Sales probably won't drop next quarter. (improbable)

_____ sales will drop next quarter.

5 It's unlikely that the competition will be as successful. (unlikely)

The competition _____ .

6 We're likely to sign a sponsorship deal at the next meeting. (probably)

_____ sign a sponsorship deal at the next meeting.

Position of adverbs and adverbial phrases

3 Put the words in brackets in the correct place in the sentences. Leave one gap blank in each sentence.

1 We will ___*probably*___ reach _____ our sales target this quarter. (probably)

2 They're on schedule, and they're _____ going to meet _____ their budget. (also)

3 Their profits _____ are _____ to increase next year. (likely)

4 We're _____ to make a loss _____ . (unlikely)

5 They _____ won't _____ accept the proposed terms of the sponsorship deal. (probably)

6 Do _____ they _____ hope to increase online sales? (also)

Listening **1** 🔊 3.01 **Listen to the financial news report. Decide if the statements are** *true* **(T) or** *false* **(F).**

1 Renault is planning to spend €1 billion to produce cars in Africa, India and Brazil. ____

2 Renault, Nissan and Mitsubishi plan to work more closely together. ____

3 Renault has clear plans to stop producing petrol cars. ____

4 Renault's plans for Brazil and India are focused on pricing. ____

5 SEAT wants to expand into Central and South America. ____

6 SEAT wants to change its image from being a young person's car. ____

7 SEAT is developing smartphone technology to work with its cars. ____

8 SEAT's most recent profit was €143.5 million. ____

2 🔊 3.02 **Complete the sentences using the phrases in the box. Then listen and check your answers.**

it's unlikely   also plans   is certain   is going to   is likely to
it's likely that   it's probable that   will probably

1 Analysts say _____ the increase in Renault's share price will continue.

2 Renault, Nissan and Mitsubishi say that their partnership _____ to become more like a single company.

3 Renault _____ launch eight new electric cars.

4 In many places, _____ petrol cars will be banned by 2040.

5 In addition to work in Brazil, India and China, Renault _____ to increase growth in Iran, Russia and North Africa.

6 Ten years from now, SEAT _____ make more than 30 percent of its sales outside of Europe.

7 One analyst said that if SEAT tries to break into the service market, _____ to succeed.

8 In the next few months, SEAT _____ launch an app.

3 **What is the speaker's aim in Exercise 1?**

a to persuade listeners to buy the automobile brands mentioned

b to share true information and facts about the two companies

c to express the importance of using technology to address climate change

Functional language

Responding to bad news

1 **Choose the correct option in the responses.**

1 The sales figures for the new line are lower than we expected.
  a I'm extremely confident that we will achieve our targets.
  b This is simply too expensive.

2 The manufacturing team are still making a lot of mistakes.
  a We just haven't made enough progress in growth areas.
  b I'm sure that we can turn this around and get production up to standard.

3 The new release isn't as popular in the market as we'd hoped.
  a It will take some time. I think we simply need to keep doing what we're doing.
  b I know. I think we should continue to focus on training.

4 The deadline's Friday, and we're not going to hit it.
  a I know. But to be fair, we're only a little behind schedule.
  b The market response was not what we were hoping for.

5 Local production is too slow and too expensive.
  a I really think it's time to try local production.
  b I'm not sure that we'll be able to continue with local production.

6 We're over budget, behind schedule and the quality is terrible.
  a Overall, things have gone really well.
  b I don't see how this can work. We have to find a new approach.

Asking for clarification and paraphrasing

2 **Choose the correct option.**

1 **A:** Did you receive the report?

  B: Yes, but there are a couple of things I'd like to *clarify / follow*. I'm having a little difficulty *following / repeating* the overall strategy.

2 **A:** Just to *catch / confirm*, what's the target amount?

  B: €250,000, I think. But let me *refer / double-check* it.

3 **A:** I have some questions about personnel. More *correctly / specifically*, who's going to be team leader?

  B: We've decided on Sonja.

4 **A:** The plans look good, but could you *confirm / remind* me what you said about timing?

  B: Sure, no problem. We're going to …

5 **A:** Hello? Sorry, the sound *went / lost* for a moment. Would you mind saying that last bit again?

  B: I said that …

6 **A:** We'll talk about budget this afternoon and schedule tomorrow morning.

  B: What you are *saying / putting differently* is that we're having two meetings?

7 **A:** I simply can't do the job without more help.

  B: If *I understood you correctly / that means*, you want to hire someone else.

Writing   Annual report summary

1 Complete the extract from a company annual report using the words in the box.

| debt   economy   forecast   invested   margins   dividend   posted   quarter   revenue   flow |

To our shareholders

The last year has seen the company making great progress, in spite of the slow-down in the global [1]_____ .
This was largely as a result of changes to exchange rates, which increased our profit [2]_____ by lowering
our manufacturing costs in China. This meant that although we were expecting about 1% growth in the final
[3]_____ , we finished with growth of 6% on the previous quarter.

The start of the year didn't give us cause to be optimistic. Sales [4]_____ in the first quarter was down
3% from the previous quarter. However, in the second quarter, our sales volume became stable. After increasing
by 1% in the third quarter, it increased by 3% in the fourth. For the year, we [5]_____ sales of $112
million, up 1.75% on the previous year. Cash [6]_____ from operations was $56 million and we
[7]_____ $35 million in capital expenditure, including opening two new retail locations in Amsterdam.
We also repaid $2 million of [8]_____ which we had borrowed for our retail expansion. As a result of our
strong performance, we were able to raise our annual [9]_____ by 4%. Last year, we launched
15 new product lines in six markets and these are doing very well. The [10]_____ for the coming year
looks promising.

---

2 Complete the notes using the headings in the box.

| Reasons for performance   Overview/Introduction   Positive aspects
Future outlook   Negative aspects |

KEY NOTES

1 _____

- Excellent progress, despite economic
  downturn in Asia

2 _____

- Decrease in cost of materials

3 _____

- Growth 3% on previous quarter
- Sales revenue at start of year was up
  3% from previous quarter
- Sales volume increase of 4% in
  final quarter.
- Cash flow from operations €52 million

- Invested €3 million in new fleet of
  delivery vehicles
- Paid off €3.5 million debt for new offices
- Annual dividend €2.30 (previous year €2.30)
- Launched completely new website – customers
  love it

4 _____

- Sales volume dropped by 2% in second and
  third quarters
- Sales €98 million – decrease of 2% from
  previous year

5 _____

- Promising forecast

---

3 Write an executive summary of about 200 words. Use:

- the structure and key notes in Exercise 2 above.

- the functional language in Exercise 2 on page 36 in the coursebook.

- some linkers: *(un)fortunately, although, despite, in spite of, after, next, last.*

4 Which sentence best describes the tone of executive summary you wrote?

a It was a difficult year, and unfortunately, next year will be difficult, too.

b The global economic situation meant that we had our best year ever.

c The year was challenging, but fortunately the future is bright.

4 ❯ Digital business

Vocabulary **Digital business and technology**

1 Choose the correct option to complete the sentences.

1 We've bought a new project management ____ and it's helping us to stay on schedule.

   a person   **b** disruptor   **c** tool

2 We don't store much information on our computers because we keep it in the ____ .

   a cloud   **b** personality   **c** visualisation

3 We're using a digital marketing ____ to handle online advertising sales.

   a prediction   **b** platform   **c** innovator

4 We use data ____ to try to learn more about our customers.

   a predictable   **b** irritating   **c** mining

5 You will find all of the information you asked for in yesterday's data ____ .

   a dump   **b** personal   **c** predictive

6 The new website is more successful, because we're seeing a 10 percent increase in ____ .

   a innovator   **b** conversion   **c** analysis

Word building – verbs, nouns and adjectives

2 Complete the definitions using the words in the box.

analyse convert irritating personalisation prediction visual

1 _____ (v) to change something into a different form, or to change something so that it can be used for a different purpose or in a different way

2 _____ (n) the act of designing or changing something so that it is suitable for a particular person

3 _____ (adj) annoying, making you feel slightly angry

4 _____ (v) to examine or think about something carefully, in order to understand it

5 _____ (n) a statement of what you think will happen

6 _____ (adj) related to seeing

3 Choose the correct option.

> **They didn't see it coming**
>
> [1]*Disruptive / Disruptor* technology approaches a problem in an industry or sector from a completely new angle. It brings some kind of [2]*innovate / innovation* to a business that has an established way of doing things. The mobile phone industry didn't [3]*anticipation / anticipate* Apple's launch of the iPhone, and not even Apple [4]*predicted / predictive* the product's early success. When Apple launched the iPhone in 2007, no one thought that more than a billion of the handsets would be sold in the next ten years, creating huge [5]*disrupt / disruption* in the mobile phone business. Initially, this was just an [6]*irritated / irritation* to mobile phone rival Blackberry, but the iPhone eventually brought Blackberry down to a 0 percent market share in 2016, an outcome that pre-iPhone [7]*analysts / analytics* hadn't seen coming.

Grammar   Zero, first and second conditionals

1 Choose the correct options.

Zero conditional

1 Unless you really *hate / hated* technology, you probably *have / had* a smartphone.

2 A translation app *was / is* useful if you *will travel / travel* internationally.

First conditional

3 Other app users *didn't / won't* know you're online if you *change / changed* your privacy settings.

4 *Unless / If* you download the app, *you'll / you'd* be able to control your heating remotely.

Second conditional

5 If I *lose / lost* my phone, I *won't / wouldn't* have anyone's contact information.

6 This app *would / will* be more useful if it *has / had* voice recognition.

2 Choose the correct explanation for each sentence.

1 Unless we start using this tool, we won't be competitive.

   a We already use this tool.   **b** We don't currently use this tool.

2 As long as they have a website, customers can buy their products online.

   a They have a website.   **b** They don't have a website.

3 If they buy ten items, they'll get one free.

   a It's not possible to get a free item.   **b** Getting a free item is a real possibility.

4 They'd be less successful if they didn't use this technology.

   a They use this technology.   **b** They don't use this technology.

5 Unless you're very good at maths, this app is very useful.

   a If you're good at maths, you need this app.   **b** If you aren't good at maths, you need this app.

6 He'll reach more customers if he takes his business online.

   a His business isn't online.   **b** His business is online.

Linkers

3 Complete the sentences using the words in the box.

if   unless   as long   provided   condition

1 _____ that you download the app, you can control your house lighting remotely.

2 _____ you update your technology regularly, you'll fall behind.

3 You can use your smartphone to edit video, _____ as you have enough memory.

4 I'll give you the test version of the app, on _____ that you don't show it to anyone.

5 You can download a free version of the app _____ you want to try it.

Reading

1 Read the article and match the correct headings with paragraphs 1–3. Two of the headings are <u>not</u> used.

a I saw it online

b Better to stay home

c Take the next right

d Out of order

e Sorry, could you repeat that?

It doesn't work yet

American inventor W. Daniel Hillis once said that technology was everything that didn't work yet. And he may have a point. If you're into using the latest digital tools and hardware, then you know that they don't always do what they're supposed to do. Here are three stories that show just how bad it can be.

1 _____

If you type your address into a satnav device or a navigation app on your phone, the software will tell you exactly how to get where you want to go. However, when a 23-year-old Canadian driver followed her satnav's instructions on a foggy night, she ended up driving into a lake! The night was dark and foggy, and the device planned a route that included taking a boat across the lake. Unfortunately, the boat wasn't there. Fortunately, the driver escaped without injury.

2 _____

Online search engines are a great way for businesses to connect with customers. But what if a search engine shows your business as 'permanently closed' even when it isn't? Businesses around the world have faced this problem with a popular search engine. According to the company, it most often occurs when a business changes location, but doesn't update its information online. If businesses realised what was going on, they could go online and fix the problem. But unless the owners know their business is listed as closed, they won't address the issue.

3 _____

When a BBC reporter tried to use a translation app on a trip to Spain, in most situations, it simply didn't work. Occasionally, as long as conditions were perfect – no noise in the background – he was able to make people understand what he wanted, but the translations never sounded natural, and were almost always confusing, or worse, funny. At one point, when the reporter was simply trying to buy a stamp, the app wouldn't translate his questions, or the words of the person selling the stamp. Finally, the shopkeeper told the reporter that he spoke English, and the app was switched off.

2 Read the article again and decide if these sentences are *true* (T) or *false* (F).

1 W. Daniel Hillis believes that the technology we use is imperfect. ____

2 According to the article, new technology rarely causes problems. ____

3 The first story is about following directions given by a device. ____

4 The driver's smartphone gave her an incorrect weather report. ____

5 In the second story, an online business sent customers the wrong products. ____

6 Sometimes, business owners don't realise that online information about their business is incorrect. ____

7 In the third story, a reporter was trying to use technology to communicate. ____

8 In the end, the technology worked very well. ____

3 What is the article mainly about?

a the danger of using technology when you travel

b problems that can occur when technology doesn't work properly

c unexpected ways to use technology

Functional language

Keeping a meeting on track

1 Complete the conversation using the phrases in the box.

> That's really outside the scope of this meeting   We can come back to it
> I'd like to stick to our agenda   Can we slow down a little
> Let her finish her point   We do need to deal with production costs

A: ¹____ and focus on marketing first.

B: But shouldn't we look at costs? Production costs have increased by 50 percent.

A: ²____ .

B: Yes, I know it is, but it's very important.

A: I agree. ³____ , but let's finish talking about marketing.

B: Yes, but production costs …

A: ⁴____ in tomorrow's meeting. For today, coming back to advertising, I asked for your responses to the initial suggestions from the ad agency. Anyone?

C: Yes, I have a couple of thoughts. I'm not sure any of the samples …

B: Right! They just weren't very …

A: ⁵____ , please. I'll come to you in a moment.

C: Thanks. As I was saying, I'm not sure any of the samples are completely suitable. There are some nice ideas there, but there was no mention of our new website, for example.

A: Yes, I noticed that too, but we did ask for the website to be right at the heart of …

B: ⁶____ ? I think I've missed something …

Reaching agreement in a negotiation

2 Put the conversation into the correct order (1–9). The first line has been done for you.

a Can we talk for a minute?   *1*

b Yes, that sounds reasonable. I suppose I can agree to that.   ____

c But it's always been free!   ____

d I'm not happy about the new charges for the staff car park. I have to drive to work, and I shouldn't have to pay for parking.   ____

e Well, maybe. But how could you imagine this working? Are there other drivers from my area? I don't know any.   ____

f How about if we try to find out? We could find out where all the drivers are based and organise a ride-sharing club. Would that work?   ____

g Sure. What's up?   ____

h I know. But that has to change. How do you feel about ride sharing with other drivers from your area?   ____

i We need to accept the fact that the maintaining the car park is a big expense for the company, but fewer than half of the staff use it.   ____

Writing   Short business proposal

1 Complete the short business proposal using the words in the box.

complaints   initial   prefer   propose   recommend   ease   solution   recover

AUTOMATED HOTEL CHECK-IN KIOSK PROPOSAL

I ¹_____ that we invest in an automated check-in system for the hotel lobby. Recently, there have been more ²_____ about waiting times at check-in. The use of an automated check-in system would help to ³_____ this issue.

Three automated customer check-in kiosks would be an excellent ⁴_____ . Most customers already make room reservations online using a credit card, so it would be easy for them to use the same credit card at check-in. And for people who ⁵_____ to speak with someone when checking-in, our reception desk would still be run as usual. Research shows that many customers like using kiosks because they find it easier and less stressful. Installing the kiosks would be a good way for us to measure our own customers' preferences.

It is expected that the ⁶_____ costs would be quite high, but as kiosks are less expensive than human employees, my research indicates that we would ⁷_____ our investment in six months. We could invest in three automated check-in kiosks before the end of the year. This would give us an overall saving which we could pass along to our customers.

In conclusion, I therefore ⁸_____ that we install three automated check-in kiosks.

2A Complete the notes using the headings in the box.

Solution to problem   Introduction or purpose statement   Conclusion
Brief summary of problem   Plan, costs and schedule

Restaurant order kiosk proposal

Aim: to reduce waiting time for food in the hotel restaurant

1 _____

- Investment in automated ordering system

2 _____

- Increasing complaints about the wait and the food quality at busy times: 7.30–8.30 a.m. and 1.00–2.00 p.m.

3 _____

- Automated food ordering kiosk in restaurant would improve customer experience
- Many customers like to see pictures of the food – this would provide that
- Five ordering kiosks could replace three waiters

- Research: reduces stress on customers not confident pronouncing unfamiliar food names
- Very easy to provide menu in several languages

4 _____

- Can start with two kiosks to test customer reaction
- Initial investment would be high, but running costs cheaper than employing waiting staff
- Savings would allow us to improve the quality of the food

5 _____

- Recommendation: two kiosks initially, and three more before the end of the year

---

B What is the writer's assumption about the restaurant's customers?

a A few customers prefer to pay in cash.

b Not all customers will speak English.

c Some customers may not want to eat meat.

3 Write a short business proposal of about 180 words. Use:

- the structure and notes in Exercise 2A above.
- the functional language in Exercise 2 on page 46 in the coursebook.

Vocabulary — Rewarding performance

1 Put the letters in the brackets in the correct order to complete the sentences.

1 We should give our new recruits enough time to _____ in their job. (d c e c u e s)

2 Our department will be holding staff _____ interviews next week. (r a s p l a p i a)

3 We tried and _____, I agree. But at least we tried! (l a f e d i)

4 Fred worked really hard and was hoping for a _____. (m o t r o n i p o)

5 Don't be afraid of _____, just keep trying. (l e f i r u a)

6 Claudia has just been _____ to senior financial adviser. (t o d e m o r p)

7 After two years, my boss recognised my _____ and gave me a bonus. (v e t s n e h a m i c e)

8 The Human Resources Manager wants to evaluate the _____ of the new rewards system. (s e s u c s c)

2 Complete the three sentences in each set using the same word in the box. Four words are <u>not</u> used.

> advance   appraisal   employment   evaluate   failure   motivation
> performance   promotion   recognition   reward   success

1 The only way to succeed is not to be afraid of _____*failure*_____.
Last year nobody received a pay rise due to the _____*failure*_____ of one of our major product lines.
Losing young, ambitious employees can lead to problems for a company or even _____*failure*_____ in certain areas.

2 Management should take the time to _____ the benefits the new recruits have brought to the company.
My proposal will also _____ the possibility of hiring recent university graduates.
We need to _____ the success of our new rewards system carefully and also take the guarantee of lifelong employment into account.

3 I was feeling frustrated because I knew that my turn for _____ and a pay rise was many years away.
Many years ago, employees were given a(n) _____ only if they had been with the company for a long time.
The company implemented a special programme that included faster _____ for junior employees, so younger staff could rise through the ranks more quickly.

4 A bonus is an extra amount of money added to an employee's wages, usually as a _____ for doing good work.
In my opinion, any _____ should be based on performance, not age.
Would you prefer to get a pay rise or have more time off as a(n) _____?

5 A lot of companies know that their _____ also depends on the performance of staff members throughout the organisation.
Our new salary model is working out well and many other companies would like to achieve the same kind of _____.
The famous businesswoman Estée Lauder once said that she never dreamed about _____, but that she worked for it.

6 Many companies realise that _____ of the work employees do often leads to increased staff motivation.
_____ means public respect and thanks for someone's work or achievements.
When staff members receive _____ for doing a good job, it makes them want to continue to perform well.

7 A performance _____ is the same as a performance review. It is a method by which the performance of an employee is evaluated.
At the beginning of my career, I found it difficult to give a(n) _____ of my own performance.
One of the goals of an employee _____ is to set targets for the future.

Grammar Linking words and concessive clauses

1 **Choose the correct option to complete the sentences.**

1 Giving pay rises often motivates workers. ____ , there isn't one particular reward system that is suitable for all situations.

   a Despite   **b** However   **c** Although   **d** Though

2 He didn't get a bonus ____ he had hit his targets.

   a although   **b** despite   **c** however   **d** even

3 Bonuses and pay rises are often awarded to encourage employees to work harder. ____ , we should remember that people very often respond positively to non-financial rewards as well.

   a In spite of   **b** Although   **c** Nevertheless   **d** Even though

4 ____ all her achievements, she didn't rise quickly through the ranks to become manager.

   a Nevertheless   **b** Although   **c** On the other hand   **d** Despite

5 On the one hand, Alex was often late for work. ____ , he always agreed to work overtime whenever he was asked to.

   a Although   **b** Despite   **c** In spite of   **d** On the other hand

6 He expected a quick promotion ____ his colleagues had told him it was highly unlikely.

   a even though   **b** nevertheless   **c** despite   **d** however

7 ____ failing to get the project off the ground, he received a reward.

   a On the one hand   **b** Despite   **c** However   **d** Nevertheless

8 ____ the performance incentives we introduced, motivation didn't increase.

   a Even though   **b** However   **c** In spite of   **d** Although

2 **Match the sentence halves.**

1 Although I had set my targets together with my manager,

2 Despite the rise in profits,

3 Even though her performance had been excellent,

4 Executives often get performance-related bonuses

5 In spite of a big pay rise,

6 Productivity didn't increase

7 On the one hand, the company offers interesting performance incentives,

8 They didn't give him a pay rise

a although, as everybody knows, their performance is often difficult to measure.

b but on the other hand, the chances of promotion are very few.

c despite acknowledging his achievements in public.

d even though the workers had been put in teams and taught how to cooperate.

e he kept complaining about lack of recognition.

f her promotion was put off until the following year.

g I soon realised I would not be able to meet them.

h nobody was awarded a bonus.

Listening 1 ◀) 5.01 **Listen to two colleagues (Boris and Livia) talking about performance and rewards. Decide if the statements are** *true* **(T) or** *false* **(F).**

1 Boris and Livia have only recently started working together. ____

2 Money is not Livia's main source of motivation at work. ____

3 Livia believes that she and all her colleagues could work even better or more. ____

4 Boris believes that people are naturally lazy. ____

5 Boris agrees that financial incentives are important. ____

6 Livia believes that competition is less important than being part of a group with common interests and objectives. ____

7 Boris believes that, more and more, companies are getting employees to compete with one another. ____

8 The 'gig economy' means that people are employed on short-term contracts and do freelance work. ____

9 Neither Boris nor Livia likes the idea of linking teachers' pay to students' examination results. ____

10 Boris believes it is easy to see how well chief executives perform. ____

2 ◀) 5.02 **Complete the sentences. Then listen and check your answers.**

1 You work hard, we all know that, and you get a fair wage. _____ , perhaps a pay rise or a bonus of some sort would motivate you to work even harder ....

2 I simply do my best. I find satisfaction in what I do, and really, _____ not all my projects are very successful, I can't see how I could possibly work better or more.

3 Financial incentives are important, of course, but _____ it would be a very sad world if we only worked to earn a better salary.

4 These days, you hardly ever hear that word, do you? It's all about productivity, competition, things like that, _____ what we need most, in my opinion, is to be part of a group with common interests and objectives.

5 Yeah ... It's happening more and more, _____ .

6 And in the meantime, so many chief executives are rewarded with huge bonuses, _____ the fact that their individual performance is so hard to measure.

3 **Tick (✓) the correct sentences.**

1 a Alex gets a fair wage. However, it's not enough to support a family of four. ☐

   b Alex doesn't get a fair wage. However, it's not enough to support a family of four. ☐

2 a Although I work hard, not all my projects are successful. ☐

   b Although I don't work hard, not all my projects are successful. ☐

3 a The last year of the business was not successful, despite an increase in their online sales. ☐

   b The last year of the business was successful, despite an increase in their online sales. ☐

4 **Choose the correct option.**

The sentences I didn't tick are not correct because there is a problem with ...

a word order.   b meaning.   c spelling.

Functional language

Responding to challenging feedback

1 Decide if each response is *defending a position* (D) or *accepting criticism* (A).

1 I don't think the estimates are realistic.

    a There's room for improvement, I agree. ____
    b I'm afraid you're not seeing the big picture. ____

2 We can't afford to waste any more time.

    a Come on. We've talked about this before. ____
    b I take on board what you're saying. ____

3 There's a real problem with quality.

    a I'm not sure what you're saying is necessarily accurate. ____
    b OK. I understand what you're saying and why. ____

4 Are you sure she's the right person for the job?

    a She is, I assure you. ____
    b I appreciate the point you're making, but not necessarily how you're making it. ____

5 This can't continue.

    a I can see your point. We may need to redesign the whole thing. ____
    b Yes, but you have to remember that we predicted this might happen. ____

Leading and participating in review meetings

2 Complete the conversation exchanges with sentences a–g.

> **a** My biggest challenge was meeting the tight deadlines.
>
> **b** Next time, we should insist on having more time.
>
> **c** Overall, it's great that we have hit all of our most important targets.
>
> **d** Well, speaking openly, I underestimated the complexity.

1 I called this meeting because I feel we need to review our progress so far. How do you think we're doing? ____

2 I'd like to hear your comments on the main challenges. ____

3 What was the main cause of this? ____

4 So how do we plan to do things differently from now on? ____

> **e** Where do you think things have gone particularly well?
>
> **f** So how do we plan to do things differently next time?
>
> **g** Which aspects of the project were the most challenging exactly?

5 ____ In terms of my own success, I managed to complete the main phases on time.

6 ____ I had to be very careful with spending in our budget, but I managed it.

7 ____ Next time, I need to dedicate more time to allocating resources.

Writing Performance review summary

1 Complete the performance review summary using the phrases in the box.

although your	however, I feel that you need to	I am impressed by your work so far
keep up	I am pleased to report that	in addition, you exhibit the skill to
nevertheless, I am confident that		you always meet the deadlines for
you demonstrate the ability to	you show a great aptitude for	

---

¹_____ the quality of your work throughout this half year has made the project very successful, meaning that you will definitely be considered for the post of team leader next year.

²_____ be flexible and constructive when difficult decisions have to be made. Being a good listener, you always consider other team members' opinions first before offering your own suggestions for solving problems.

³_____ encourage, support and motivate the other team members. The feedback I get from them is consistently positive.

Overall, ⁴_____ and your communication skills in particular. ⁵_____ communicating professionally and confidently in face-to-face situations with both internal and external partners and clients. ⁶_____ develop your written communication skills further.

⁷_____ emails generally meet the required standards, your reports often need to be more accurate and better organised. I appreciate the fact that ⁸_____ submitting reports, but this should not be at the expense of accuracy. ⁹_____ you will easily be able to develop your report writing skills by attending one of our staff training courses.

¹⁰_____ the good work!

---

2 Mark the phrases and sentences *PC* (positive comments) or *CC* (constructive criticism).

1 … could be improved. ____

2 Furthermore, you have displayed considerable (problem-solving) skills … ____

3 However, this can be easily resolved (by … / with …) ____

4 I am very pleased … ____

5 This can sometimes lead to unavoidable delays. ____

6 You and your team must also be praised for … ____

7 You have been able to … ____

8 You should try to … ____

3 Write a performance review summary. Write 170–220 words. Use:

- the notes below (add relevant extra information where appropriate).

- the functional language in Exercises 1 and 2 above.

Remember to:

- open the text in a positive way.

- include all the positive comments as well as constructive criticism.

- suggest a possible solution where appropriate.

- close on a positive note.

✓ great achievements over the year (latest project completed on schedule and within budget!)
✓ great team worker + communicator (listens actively / gives clear advice whenever requested, etc.)
  – great feedback from everyone
✓ learning advanced computer skills (very successful!)
✓ good organisational skills overall (but see below!)
✗ sometimes has difficulty working under pressure → Solution: prioritise things to do on a given day or in a week?
✗ not always able to attend meetings regularly → Why? lots of demands on time → Solution: talk to line manager

Vocabulary Business ethics

1 Use the clues to complete the word tree.
The last letter of each word has been given.

1 _____l fashion means creating and wearing
beautiful clothes that aren't made in sweatshops.

2 A fashion _____r tries to create clothes that
people will want to wear.

3 New clothing designs are usually presented at
a fashion _____w.

4 Some consumers prefer to shop at a fashion
_____r that sells ethical clothing.

5 Many people want to improve the lives of
workers in the fashion _____y.

2 Choose one word from each box to make collocations. Then complete
the sentences.

clothing   fair trade   moral   unethical
approach   brands   conduct   cotton

1 Top _____ compete to keep creating high fashion at low prices.

2 Campaigners have criticised the clothing industry for its _____ .

3 Consumers like clothes made from _____ because they know the
producers have been paid a fair price.

4 Truly ethical businesses believe in a _____ to commerce.

ethically   low   environmental   tough
conditions   pay   impact   sourced

5 Factory workers too often receive _____ rates.

6 Fashion brands should also consider the _____ on our planet.

7 When materials are _____ , everyone who makes them is treated
fairly.

8 The _____ in factories include dangerous equipment and lack of light
and fresh air.

3 Choose the correct option.

> **It's getting better**
>
> Looking ¹*up / across* the fashion industry, companies have come under more and
> more pressure to end the practice of making clothes in sweatshops with dangerous
> ²*conditioning / conditions*. For years, people both inside and outside the industry have
> campaigned ³*against / of* manufacturers that keep costs down by keeping workers' pay
> as low as possible, and save money by not providing safe workplaces. As consumers
> become more ⁴*aware / beware* of the problem, some are helping the situation by
> making buying choices that have an impact ⁵*on / against* unethical companies. It's
> increasingly important for companies that are accused ⁶*for / of* unethical practices to
> take responsibility ⁷*of / for* their actions, and to treat workers fairly.

Grammar Third conditional

1 **Choose the correct option.**

1 We didn't use local ingredients, but if we had, we *could have advertised / advertised* the restaurant as having low carbon emissions.

2 If they *hadn't paid / aren't paying* our workers a reasonable wage, they wouldn't have been an ethical company.

3 *Would you have had / Did you have* more support from the community if your employees had done some volunteer work locally?

4 If we *recycled / had recycled* our waste, we wouldn't have had to pay to transport it away from the factory.

5 Your shareholders *have / would have* been upset if you had had any more losses.

6 If we *hadn't given / don't give* some of our profits to charity, our workers would have complained.

2 **Complete the sentences with the correct form of the verbs in brackets to make third conditional sentences.**

1 If the company _____ (not / be) ethical, I wouldn't have invested in it.

2 You would have had workplace equality in the last few years if you _____ (have) more female managers.

3 If the business had been responsible in those days, then it _____ (pay) its workers better than it did.

4 Local people _____ (be) unhappy if we hadn't donated to the community.

5 If the business _____ (grow) more slowly, it might not have made mistakes.

6 You would have reduced your carbon footprint if you _____ (cycle) to work last year.

3 **Complete the sentences to explain what would or would not have happened.**

1 They didn't pay their tax. They got in trouble.

If they _____ their tax, they _____ in trouble.

2 The company made their clothes in sweatshops. They had bad publicity.

The company _____ bad publicity if they _____ their clothes in sweatshops.

3 He gave his wife and kids jobs. He was accused of nepotism.

If he _____ his wife and kids jobs, he _____ accused of nepotism.

4 She presented a sustainability statement. The share price went up.

If she _____ the sustainability statement, the share price _____ up.

5 You didn't reduce your business travel. Your carbon footprint didn't get smaller.

Your carbon footprint _____ smaller if you _____ your business travel.

Reading **1** Read the article and complete it with sentences a–h.

a Let's look at some projects that Triodos Bank has funded.

b Instead, he'd been in and out of jail for most of his adult life.

c But it wasn't always that way.

d Why three-way?

e There's also an ecological garden where students grow organic vegetables.

f According to its founders, it supports a global society and teaches people to be aware, happy and healthy.

g This is another example of Triodos working to make the world a better place.

h When it was reported that the tin-mining industry was ruining Indonesia's environment, Triodos convinced Philips to join their effort and take responsibility for its environmental impact.

The triple-bottom-line bank

The Greek expression *tri hodos* means 'three-way approach', and that's where Triodos Bank gets its name. ¹____ People, planet, profit. Founded in 1980 in Zeist, Netherlands, the ethical bank takes what it calls a fresh approach to banking, offering accounts to businesses and individuals who want their money to be used as a force for good in society. Triodos is happy to lend money to businesses and projects that make the world a better place, and refuses to do business with organisations that are unethical or damage people or the planet. What does that look like in the real world? ²____

The Together Group, Scotland

A construction worker known only as J has a good job with a steady income. ³____ J says that if he hadn't been given a chance by an organisation called The Together Group, he would have had nothing. J came from a troubled background and, aged thirty, had never had a job. ⁴____ The Together Group – with finance from Triodos – creates jobs for people leaving prison by giving them skills for the construction industry, as well as a social network and lots of support.

Escuela Ideo, Spain

Triodos believes that good education is a basic element of human development. If the bank hadn't provided financial support, the Ideo School in Madrid, Spain wouldn't have been able to offer an alternative, more positive education to young people. ⁵____ Students are encouraged to come to school by bicycle rather than being driven, and the school's power comes from renewable resources. ⁶____ Triodos finances schools because it believes education serves people for their entire life.

Philips in the Netherlands and Indonesia

Dutch electronics manufacturer Philips buys the metal tin from producers in Indonesia. ⁷____ With other investors, the bank began working to improve conditions in Indonesia. If Philips and other companies hadn't agreed to work on improvements, the horrible impact of the tin-mining industry would have continued. ⁸____

With more than €4.5 billion in assets, Triodos has proven that the triple bottom line works.

2 Read the article again and choose the correct option.

1 Triodos first opened in *Scotland / Spain / the Netherlands*.

2 Triodos wants to do business only with companies that are *educational / ethical / traditional*.

3 Before they joined The Together Group, its members used to be *police officers / students / criminals*.

4 In the Ideo School, there is an ecological garden where students grow *environmental / organic / renewable* vegetables.

5 Triodos worked to stop *sweatshops / tin-mining / environmental damage* in Indonesia.

6 Triodos brought about a change with Philips *through cooperation / with a lawsuit / with consumer protest*.

3 Which sentence best describes the article?

a It defines a problem, then gives the solution.

b It makes a statement, then gives evidence to support it.

c It asks a question, then provides the answer.

Functional language

Voicing and responding to concerns

1 Choose the correct option to complete the responses.

1

> Do you think they can pay the bill?

> *I'm afraid / I'm playing devil's advocate* they're struggling with cash flow problems.

2

> Do you think we should cancel the order?

> Yes. I'm *concerned / for certain* they aren't going to deliver on time.

3

> We've agreed to deliver a month before the deadline.

> *I don't want to worry you / I'm not entirely sure* that was a good idea.

4

> He says he's going to increase the price.

> *This information isn't confirmed / To be honest*, we can't let him do that.

5

> Did you say you think we should ask Darius for help?

> *It's just a thought / No, I'm sorry*. I could be wrong.

Selling a product or service

2 What would you say? Match situations 1–8 with sentences a–h.

1 You want to introduce what your company sells. ____

2 You want to explain how a product helps clients. ____

3 You want to show personal conviction in a product. ____

4 You want to check a client's needs. ____

5 You want to request feedback on what you said. ____

6 You want to explore possible blockers to a sale. ____

7 You want to invite further questions from a client. ____

8 You want to focus on future actions. ____

a Could this software be useful for you?

b We specialise in software solutions for medium-sized companies.

c I am absolutely certain that we have what you need.

d Are there any other questions I can answer right now?

e How does that sound?

f So, how about if I come and show you the product?

g Our solutions enable you to communicate with clients more effectively.

h Is budget a major consideration for you?

Writing Company newsletter

1 Complete the text with one word in each gap.

Neighbourhood
tidy-up success _____

As you know, our company is participating in the 'Good Neighbour' programme.
¹_____ a result our Clean Streets has picked up litter in our area and across town three times so far this month. CEO Joelle Van Espen says, 'If this community had not welcomed our business and made us feel at home here, we wouldn't have become a successful company. ²_____ , we feel it's important for us to give something practical back to the community, and to show our pride in this place.'

Right now, the Clean Streets team are working hard to reach our goal of two tonnes of litter by the end of this week. But we've got one more month to go and a goal of three tonnes, ³_____ we are looking for more volunteers to join us for the next two weekends. We're encouraging employees to bring the whole family.

The Clean Streets project has been so successful ⁴_____ we are going to launch at least one new project in the new year. Next week, we will put a suggestions page on the office intranet where you can put forward any ideas that you may have for how we can give more back to the community. So start thinking!

2 Read the notes. Then match each of the headings (1–3) with two notes (a–f).

1 Recent news: ____ , ____

2 Current news: ____ , ____

3 Future plans: ____ , ____

Notes on Education Outreach – part of the 'Good Neighbour' programme

a *Plan: work experience programme for local high-school students – local students get work experience, we identify possible employees*

b *CEO Joelle Van Espen quotation from a presentation last week: 'If I hadn't had the opportunity to go to university, I would never have started this company. We need to support education.'*

c *Olivia in Human Resources will answer any questions you have and take the names of volunteers*

d *Currently looking for volunteers – visit schools, talk to students about the programme, explain the application process (also try to make them aware of the work we do here, career possibilities)*

e *Education Outreach team met with representatives from three local high schools, offered financial help with university expenses for bright students who might struggle to pay for college*

f *This month: scheduling more meetings with school heads*

---

3 Write an internal company newsletter of about 200 words. Use:

· the structure and notes in Exercise 2 above.

· the functional language in Exercise 2 on page 66 in the coursebook.

4 What is the main purpose of the internal company newsletter you wrote?

a to help management gather information on workers' interests and activities

b to attract investors by showing them the company's moral approach

c to encourage employees to feel positive about work and the company

7 Time management

Vocabulary   Managing time

1 Choose the correct option.

In my company, we have a team meeting every Monday morning to [1] *set / take* goals for the week. Each of us has to [2] *measure / identify* key priorities, and [3] *maximise / schedule* jobs accordingly. If something can wait until next week, we shouldn't [4] *allocate / use* resources to it this week. The point is to waste as little time as possible and to [5] *maximise / set* efficiency. We all know each other's schedule because we [6] *schedule / use* digital calendars and share them with the team. We also [7] *allocate / measure* the time we spend on each project, so we know exactly how long jobs take. This helps with planning future projects. We talk about time and efficiency a lot, but our boss also reminds us to [8] *identify / take* a break every few hours.

2 Complete the conversations using the phrases in the box.

ahead of time   at a time   at the same time   by the time   on time   out of time

1 A: Are we going to be _____ for the sales presentation?

   B: No, I'm afraid we're going to be a few minutes late.

2 A: Can I ask another question?

   B: Sorry, no. We're _____ .

3 A: There are about twenty people who want to ask a question.

   B: That's OK. We'll take them one _____ .

4 A: I can't drive and talk on the phone _____ . Will you take this call?

   B: Sure, no problem.

5 A: Here's the report you wanted by Friday.

   B: Wow! Two days _____ ! That's great!

6 A: Did you tell Davina the meeting was cancelled?

   B: Yes, but _____ I finally reached her, she was already on the train.

3 Match the questions (1–6) with the responses (a–f).

1 Are we in time for the presentation? ____

2 Are you working overtime? ____

3 Do you think I'm wasting my time? ____

4 How much time did you spend on this? ____

5 What do you mean by 'time is money'? ____

6 Can you make time for a meeting tomorrow? ____

a Yes, I have a deadline tomorrow.

b About six hours – not very long.

c Yes. It starts in five minutes.

d Sure. How about right after lunch?

e We don't have long to hit our targets before the deadline today and you should be out selling.

f No, I think if you keep asking, you'll eventually get an answer.

Grammar Adverbials and time expressions

1 Complete the table using the words and phrases in the box.

> always frequently hardly ever never now and then
> rarely seldom sometimes usually

100%	I	1 _____	work overtime during busy periods.
	We	normally 2 _____ 3 _____	
	They	often	have lunch at their desks.
	I go home early on a Friday afternoon		from time to time. 4 _____ .
	I	occasionally	go home early on a Friday afternoon.
	She	5 _____ 6 _____ 7 _____	leaves the office before seven o'clock.
	You	8 _____ almost never	do administrative work.
0%	He	9 _____	works at weekends.

2 Match the words in bold in 1–6 with meanings a–f.

1 She sits at her desk **all day**. ____

2 We can arrange the product presentation for **any day**. ____

3 I wake up at six o'clock **every day**. ____

4 We **sometimes** work until midnight. ____

5 You should arrive for the meeting at nine o'clock **at the latest**. ____

6 He has **recently** started leaving the office at five o' clock every day. ____

a occasionally

b on an unspecified day

c from Monday to Sunday

d no later than the time mentioned

e not long ago

f from morning till evening

3 Choose the correct option.

1 *Almost never / Occasionally*, we have meetings at lunch time.

2 They *never / from time to time* work on a Sunday.

3 *I didn't like at first / At first, I didn't like* the suggestion of a seven o'clock start.

4 *Always, she's / She's always* on her break at two in the afternoon.

5 He doesn't *normally work / work normally* on Wednesdays.

6 We are *in a few hours going home / going home in a few hours*.

7 *Hardly ever I / I hardly ever* work later than 6.30 p.m.

8 Do you go to visit *customers now and then / now and then customers*?

9 *Rarely I'm / I'm rarely* late for work.

10 *He's from time to time / From time to time he's* in the office on a Saturday.

Listening   **1** ◄)) 7.01   Listen to four people talking about their working hours. Choose the correct option.

Speaker 1

1 She leaves work on time *now and then / frequently*.

2 She *always / never* has too much work to do.

Speaker 2

3 His working hours have *never / recently* decreased.

4 He *almost always / rarely* works forty hours or more in a week.

Speaker 3

5 She *occasionally / often* goes to work in other companies' offices.

6 She *never / seldom* works at weekends.

Speaker 4

7 He *rarely / normally* works overtime in the office.

8 He *seldom / frequently* socialises as part of his job.

2 Listen again and choose the correct option.

Speaker 1

1 What time does her work day begin?

   a 8.00   **b** 8.30   **c** 8.45   **d** 9.00

2 What time could she finish her work if she managed her time well?

   a 4.00   **b** 5.00   **c** 6.00   **d** 7.00

Speaker 2

3 What change was made in his office?

   a overtime forbidden   **b** longer lunches   **c** pay reduced   **d** shorter meetings

4 How do the employees feel about the changes?

   a unhappy   **b** pleased   **c** uncertain   **d** angry

Speaker 3

5 What does she help companies improve?

   a administration   **b** management   **c** productivity   **d** communication

6 What does she do every day?

   a has lunch   **b** evening work   **c** wastes time   **d** leaves work early

Speaker 4

7 How many hours per night does he often spend socialising?

   a 3–4   **b** 4–5   **c** 5–6   **d** 6–7

8 How does he usually feel when he socialises for work?

   a very nervous   **b** bored   **c** happy   **d** not completely relaxed

3 Listen again. Tick (✓) the two statements that are supported by what the speakers said. Which speaker (1–4) made the supporting comments?

a Working longer hours is usually the best way to be productive. ☐ ___

b If you work more efficiently, you can reduce your working hours. ☐ ___

c Entertaining clients may look like an easy job, but it's actually hard work. ☐ ___

d Everyone should expect to work overtime sometimes. ☐ ___

Functional language

Discussing priorities

1 Match 1-6 with a-f to complete the conversations.

1 Please prioritise this. It's important. ____

2 I've received your email. Is it urgent? ____

3 When do you think you'll be able to give me a definite answer? ____

4 Did you get my message? ____

5 I've seen your email and will respond by the end of the day. ____

6 Let me know when you'll get a chance to give me your feedback. ____

a I need a response by tomorrow morning.

b I'll know before the end of the week.

c OK. Thanks.

d Yes. I'm sorry for not getting back to you sooner.

e I am overloaded right now. Can I get back to you tomorrow?

f I know it is. I'll get back to you within the hour.

Dealing with difficulties in negotiations

2A Choose the correct option to complete the conversations.

1

> I don't think the trip to New York is a good idea.

> ____ you definitely won't go?

a How about   b So, what you're saying is   c What that means is

2

> ____ that Milo has to go.

> Yes, but does it have to be me who tells him?

a I think we can both agree   b In your opinion   c We're going to have to go the extra mile

3

> We had to do this because of the planned changes to the company structure.

> ____ a bit more now.

a What that means exactly is   b In other words, you don't want to   c I understand your position

4

> ____ starting next month?

> Yes, that would work for me.

a How would you feel about   b What that means exactly is that   c So what you're saying is

5

> I'm afraid I'm going to be out of the office all next week.

> ____ we need to find someone to cover for you.

a From your point of view   b This is a good thing   c What that means exactly is that

B Match the completed sentences in Exercise 2A with categories a-e.

a Refer to common understanding ____

b Make suggestions / Be positive   _4a_

c State necessary action ____

d Acknowledge the other person's perspective ____

e Check your understanding ____

Writing An email giving reasons

1 Complete the email about missing a deadline using the words in the box.

> deadline   due   inconvenience   problem   propose   reason   reassess   solve

Hi Henri,

I'm really sorry to tell you that we've hit a(n) ¹ _____ with the new computer network. Consequently, I don't think we'll be able to meet the ² _____ set for the installation.

The main ³ _____ for this is that the supplier is unable to deliver all 60 of the computer workstations we need. In addition, there is a problem running your database software on the new computers ⁴ _____ to a compatibility issue. The software manufacturer is going to have to do an update, which they're working on. We're currently looking at alternatives.

The supplier can deliver 40 workstations now and has promised to send an additional 20 by the end of the month. I ⁵ _____ that we try to find another supplier who can give us the additional 20 workstations in the next few days and re-schedule the network installation for two weeks later. This will give the software manufacturer time to ⁶ _____ the software problem and issue an update. The delay is going to have a knock-on effect for the removal of the old network, so we may need to ⁷ _____ our schedule. I apologise for the ⁸ _____ caused and promise to sort it out as soon as possible. I'll keep you updated at all times.

Best regards,

Alexandra

2 Choose the best meaning for the expressions in bold from the email in Exercise 1.

1 '**I don't think we'll be able to** meet the deadline.' means:

    a *We won't be able to*, but it sounds softer / less direct.

    b *We may be able to*, but the writer isn't sure.

2 '**We may need to** reassess our schedule.' means:

    a *We probably don't need to*, but there's a chance we will.

    b *We probably need to*, but is more polite / less direct.

3 'I promise to sort it out **as soon as possible**.' means:

    a I don't know exactly when, but I'll do my best.

    b I know when, but I don't want to tell you.

3 Label the notes with *Problems*, *Reasons* and *Actions*.

1 _____	2 _____	3 _____
• Supplier unable to deliver all 30 security cameras. • There was an update in the manufacturer's electronic door locks.	• Supplier can deliver 20 cameras now and 10 by the end of next week. • Reconsider electronic door locks or replace all employees' ID cards.	• Installation of new office security system (including security cameras) will be late. • Current employee ID cards won't work with new door system.

4 Write an email of about 200 words explaining reasons for missing a deadline. Use the following:

- the structure of the email in Exercise 1 above (introduce the problem, explain the reason, outline the required action).

- the notes in Exercise 3 above.

- the functional language in Exercise 2 on page 76 in the coursebook.

Vocabulary Change management

1 Complete the sentences using the words in the box.

> communicate   efficient   keep growing   the move   to move   weigh up

1 For a company to get bigger – and to _____ – change is necessary.

2 Companies often need _____ to a larger site.

3 It is essential to _____ the risks and benefits of any change.

4 If you don't _____ with staff about what to expect, it can cause problems.

5 On the day of _____ , you need to be organised so nothing gets lost.

6 If you're quick and _____ , you can set up a new office in a day or two.

2 Complete the words in the word tree to find the hidden word. Use the definitions to help you.

1 when a group of people work effectively together

2 to succeed in dealing with a difficult problem or situation

3 the possibility that something bad, unpleasant, or dangerous may happen

4 worried or nervous about something that you are going to do, or about the future

5 to discuss something with someone so that you can make a decision together

6 an advantage, improvement or help that you get from something

The hidden word means: the level of confidence and positive feelings that people have, especially people who work together, who belong to the same team

3 Choose the correct option.

> **Managing change in the natural health and beauty business**
>
> Romy Fraser is a ¹*successful / success* businesswoman – founder of Neal's Yard Remedies, a natural health-and-beauty product maker in Covent Garden, London. The company sells its products in at least two dozen countries, but at the beginning, running an international business wasn't Romy's ²*plan / planning*. In 1981, a friend asked her to set up the shop as part of his natural food business, and she was ³*engaged / engaging* by the idea. She took a financial ⁴*risky / risk*, borrowing £18,000 to open the shop. After three years, the loan was paid off, and Romy took another loan to ⁵*improvement / improve* their production facilities, opening a small factory in another part of London, and also another shop. The ⁶*benefits / beneficial* of the expansion were immediate. To grow the business further, Romy and some of her employees created and ⁷*implementation / implemented* a franchise agreement, and the business grew even more. Through all of the amazing change and growth of the business, Romy has proved to be extremely ⁸*adapt / adaptable*, running a tiny shop and then a successful international business, all with great skill.

Grammar   Reported speech and reporting verbs

1 **Choose the correct option.**

1 'I enjoyed all of the subjects I studied at school,' said Janos to Greta.

Janos [1] *told / said* Greta that he had enjoyed all of the subjects he [2] *studies / had studied* at school.

2 Agata said, 'My first year of university was really challenging.'

Agata said that [3] *my / her* first year of university [4] *had been / were* really challenging.

3 'I like to plan things in advance,' said Sam.

Sam said that he [5] *liked / had liked* to plan things in advance.

4 Paola said to Juan, 'David is going to have to find a new job.'

Paola [6] *told to / told* Juan that David [7] *was going to have to find / had found* a new job.

5 Franco said to me, 'Some changes are more stressful than others.'

Franco told me that some changes [8] *were / had been* more stressful than others.

6 Sylvana said, 'My family and friends supported me a lot.'

Sylvana [9] *told / said* that her family and friends [10] *support / had supported* her a lot.

2 **Complete the sentences using the words in the box.**

advised   complained   confirmed   informed   promised   suggested

1 The client _____ to pay the invoice on time.

2 The factory manager _____ moving to a larger building.

3 When we asked, she _____ that she had already resigned.

4 The workers _____ that the new offices were too small.

5 The supplier _____ us that the order would be a few days late.

6 My brother _____ me to study engineering.

3 **Choose the correct option.**

1 James said, 'This thing is ancient! You have to buy a new computer.'

   a James insisted that I buy a new computer.

   b James suggested buying a new computer.

2 Begonia said, 'I will never be late for a meeting again!'

   a Begonia confirmed that she wouldn't be late for any meetings in the future.

   b Begonia promised that she wouldn't be late for any meetings in the future.

3 Matthew said, 'My new office is too small, and I really don't like it.'

   a Matthew informed us that his new office was small.

   b Matthew complained that his new office was too small.

4 Lena said to Adam, 'I think you should study architecture.'

   a Lena advised Adam to study architecture.

   b Lena confirmed that Adam was going to study architecture.

5 Pietro said, 'Maybe you should call Elena.'

   a Pietro insisted on calling Elena.

   b Pietro suggested that I call Elena.

Reading **1** **Read the article and label paragraphs 1-6 with the correct headings a-f.**

    a Make a plan
    d Measure the results

    b Decide what you want to change
    e Introduce the change to the team

    c Make the change
    f Keep the change going

Six steps to managing change in a company

In business as in life, change is constant, but rarely easy. But that doesn't mean you should be afraid of it. We spoke to three top managers – Mandy Wong, Heinz Müller and Maria Silva – to find out how they manage change in the workplace. They identified six key steps.

1 _____

Mandy suggested looking at your current position and asking yourself what's working and what isn't. She said, 'Imagine how you want things to be different. At this stage, make sure that you can clearly explain to yourself why the change will be a real improvement. What's going to get better? If you can't make it clear to yourself, you won't be able to sell it to other people.'

2 _____

Heinz advised managers to tell the entire team what they had in mind. He said, 'If there are decisions that need to be made, invite team members to make as many as possible together. If people feel they are part of the decision-making process, it will win everyone's support – and you'll need all the support you can get. Also, this is the time when you need to address any worries that people might have about the change.'

3 _____

Maria informed us that once she's come up with an idea and told the team about it, she works with the team and decides what people's roles and responsibilities are during the change. 'At this time,' she said, 'you need to make a clear schedule for the change and be sure to communicate the plans to everyone who's involved or will be affected by the change.'

4 _____

Mandy insisted that it's very important at this stage to make the change according to the schedule you made, and with everyone taking care of their own role and responsibilities. She adds, 'You should also support everyone during the change and make sure people have what they need. Try to make the benefit of the change obvious as soon as possible.'

5 _____

Heinz complained that change is never easy. He said, 'After you've made a change, your work isn't yet finished. I assure you; things rarely go perfectly, so you will need to identify and solve any problems that have arisen. And as people start to get used to a new way of doing things, everyone has to make sure they don't return to old habits. Continue to focus on the benefits of the change.'

6 _____

Maria promised that change always creates a learning opportunity. She says, 'Once people are used to the new way of doing things, it's a good time to reflect on what has actually changed. Compare your actual results with what you imagined at the beginning.' And is it important to learn from mistakes? 'Definitely. I always learn from the things that didn't go as planned.'

2 **For each sentence, write _Maria_, _Mandy_ or _Heinz_.**

    Who ...

    1 informed us that the workers should be able to make choices when there is change?   _____

    2 confirmed that mistakes can be good teachers?   _____

    3 advised managers to follow the timetable very closely.   _____

    4 insisted that you must understand exactly what you want to change?   _____

    5 promised that when there is change, there will always be challenges?   _____

    6 suggested that it's important for people to know what they're supposed to do?   _____

3 **Tick (✓) the three statements which are supported by the article. Underline the sections of the text that support your answers.**

    a Managers often make changes that don't actually improve anything. ☐

    b Change can be stressful for employees. ☐

    c Sometimes change creates unexpected results. ☐

    d If you give employees a choice, there will probably be serious disagreements. ☐

    e Change can be challenging, but it's often beneficial. ☐

    f Mistakes are bad and should be avoided. ☐

Functional language

Language for coaching and mentoring

1 Choose the correct response.

1 I don't know anything about the market.
- a You should get some further training.
- b How do you think you could achieve this?

2 Do you think you should look at other options?
- a You should get some more details.
- b That's a good idea, I think.

3 I'm not sure I'm ready to lead a product launch.
- a What are your options?
- b If I were you, I'd take this opportunity.

4 There's a lot to think about.
- a Yes, but you need to make a decision soon.
- b I think it would be best for you to think about it.

5 What should I do?
- a How do you think you could best approach this?
- b I can't tell you what to do, but I can help you decide.

6 Have you considered doing some research?
- a That would be a great starting point.
- b And have you thought about getting some support?

7 What are your concerns?
- a Time and money.
- b Thanks for your support.

Leading a brainstorming session

2 Group sentences a–h under the correct headings 1–8.

a There is no right or wrong – all contributions are valid.

b Can you elaborate on that?

c We're here today to address the challenges presented by the new government regulations.

d Let's go with that as a plan of action.

e Adding to that idea, we could also share our main findings in an online document.

f Are we all agreed that this will be an effective method?

g How would you like to categorise them?

h These opening questions will enable us to identify what we consider most important.

1 Define the goal _____

2 Start with questions and statements about the issue _____

3 Collect as many ideas as possible _____

4 Ask for ideas about procedure _____

5 Ask people to give more details _____

6 Build on the ideas of others _____

7 Discuss and evaluate _____

8 Make a decision _____

Writing Press release

1 Complete the press release using the words in the box.

> announced   assured   expected   informed   promised   regretted

---

Hi-Watt Motors announces factory closure

Electric carmaker Hi-Watt Motors has ¹_____ plans to close its manufacturing facility near Mexico City by the end of this year. The factory, first opened three years ago, has produced about 1,500 luxury electric cars, but the company says that strong competition in the luxury electrical vehicle market has forced them to re-think their strategy and to cut costs.

The management team and fifty workers at the factory have been ²_____ of the decision and a timeline has been laid out and redundancy packages agreed. Hi-Watt is currently trying to sell the facility, which was purpose-built by the company.

Hi-Watt is determined to stay competitive in the electric car market and intends to avoid over-stretching in the future. CEO Harald Dürkop said he ³_____ the closure, which was partly caused by international currency fluctuations. In addition, a general drop in the price of luxury electric vehicles affected the business. He insisted that the company is strong enough and has the resources to face the current crisis.

It's ⁴_____ that the factory will continue to operate for several more weeks to fulfil existing orders. Mr Dürkop ⁵_____ current owners that Hi-Watt will continue to produce spare parts, and ⁶_____ to honour service contracts for existing Hi-Watt cars. According to Dürkop, the closure is a sign of the company's strength and desire to survive, rather than its weakness.

---

2 Complete the notes using the headings in the box.

> Further details   Future promises   News and key facts   Quotation and apology

---

Notes – Mobile phone maker SmaHan press release

1 _____

- plan to close research and development centre near Mumbai by end of week
- opened two years ago, came up with design for SH-X, SmaHan's most recent model
- SH-X performed below expectations in the market

2 _____

- management team and engineers informed, redundancy packages agreed
- SmaHan will pay for the rental property until the lease ends in three months
- will leave earlier if can find someone to take over

3 _____

- determined to continue offering low-price, fashionable smartphones and intend to learn from the mistakes made in producing the SH-X
- CEO Jinsoo Park: 'I regret the closure. It was partly caused by my own failure to choose the development team carefully enough. All of the engineers at the facility are very talented, but the company failed to help them understand its vision clearly.'

4 _____

- expect none of the Mumbai-based team will return to the office
- Mr Park: 'We will continue to support the SmaHan SH-X. We will issue software updates in the near future that will solve some of the problems that users have been complaining about.'

---

3 Write a press release of about 200 words. Use:

- the structure of the press release in Exercise 1 above.
- the notes in Exercise 2 above.
- the functional language in Exercise 2 on page 86 in the coursebook.

Pronunciation

Unit 1

1.1 Stress in compound nouns

1 Write the words in the correct place in the table, according to their stress pattern.

| car loan   card payment   company practices   credit card debt   customer support representative |
| dress code   fund transfers   job application   minimum salary   pay structure   working atmosphere |

Stress on the first word	Stress on the second word

2 ◀) P1.01 Listen and check. Then listen again and practise saying the words.

1.2 Auxiliary verbs in the Future Continuous and Future Perfect Simple

1 Before you listen, circle the examples of *will* that can be written as the contracted form *'ll*.

1 By the middle of the next century, workplace culture will have changed drastically.

2 We hope our employees care whether or not we will be making a profit in the future as our success depends on it.

3 Within a few years, these new initiatives will have made a real difference.

4 My company just announced that next year they will be changing the dress code to business casual.

5 There's a lot of discussion about what companies will be doing in the future to keep their employees motivated.

6 The Managing Board has announced that in order to retain young staff members, they will have implemented a scheme for swifter promotions by the beginning of next year.

2 ◀) P1.02 Listen to the sentences in Exercise 1 and underline where you hear /l/ instead of *will*.

3 ◀) P1.03 Listen to some of the sentences again and underline where you hear /əv/ instead of *have*.

1 By the middle of the next century, workplace culture will have changed drastically.

2 Within a few years, these new initiatives will have made a real difference.

3 The Managing Board has announced that in order to retain young staff members, they will have implemented a scheme for swifter promotions by the beginning of next year.

4 Practise saying the sentences in Exercise 3.

5 ◀) P1.04 Listen and practise. Pay attention to the contracted form of *will* /l/ and weak form of *have* /əv/.

> **Business news**
> It is expected that the market will have recovered by close of business today.
> They'll be hoping for a new investor who'll have the experience to turn the company around.
> By that time, I hope they will have accepted our bid.
> It'll be some time before all the markets will have recovered.

Unit 2

2.1 Stressing key words in sentences

1 Decide which word(s) you would stress for the different meanings of each sentence.

1 The mentor is there to act as a guide and offer support.

Which word(s) would you stress to emphasise:

a who has the role?

b what the role is?

2 Training and development is a critical function in a modern business.

Which word(s) would you stress to emphasise:

a what is critical?

b the importance of training and development?

3 Because the world is constantly changing, we all need to learn to adapt.

Which word(s) would you stress to emphasise:

a what we need to do?

b why we need to do it?

2 🔊 P2.01 Listen and check. Then listen again and practise saying the sentences.

2.4 Linking between words

1 Read the text below and put the connected phrases in the table, according to the type of linking between the words. The first one has been done for you.

> Facilitation in a professional context is the art of leading discussions and meetings. It is a set of skills which guides people to discuss openly and productively. In practice, it means confirming the objective‿of‿a discussion, helping people feel confident to‿express their‿ideas, helping people to listen to‿each other, ensuring all ideas are considered, and supporting people to come to the best decision. Without effective facilitation, meetings can become a waste of time. Most meetings have‿a facilitator but are‿often more‿effective‿if all the people at the meeting share‿responsibility and help facilitate the discussion.

/v/	/w/	/r/
objective of		

2 🔊 P2.02 Listen and check. Then listen again and practise saying the phrases.

Unit 3

3.3 The letter 't'

1 ◀ᴾ3.01 **Listen to each group and decide which 't' is pronounced differently from the others.**

1 **a** just a little issue   **c** confident and optimistic

   b the cheapest option   **d** invest in new technology

   ____ is different because it is a glottal stop. The other 't's are linked to the following vowels.

2 **a** the next full project meeting   **c** just like I predicted

   b we can't run a project like this   **d** just to see what's going on

   ____ is different because the 't' is pronounced. The other 't's are dropped.

3 **a** I'm sure that we can turn this around   **c** think about it

   b but only if we act now   **d** a lot of money

   ____ is different because the 't' is dropped. The other 't's can be heard.

4 **a** not a bad result   **c** I'm going out there

   b under target   **d** quite constructive

   ____ is different because the 't' is pronounced as /t/. The other 't's are dropped.

5 **a** just try   **c** the next full project meeting

   b you don't trust them   **d** over budget a little

   ____ is different because 't' is pronounced and linked to the following vowel. The other 't's are dropped.

3.4 Strong and weak forms of *that*

1 **Before you listen, decide if the words in italics will be in the *strong form* (S) or *weak form* (W).**

1 *That* wasn't what I meant.   _W_

2 Could you say *that* again?   ____

3 Do *that* again, and you'll regret it!   ____

4 Could you repeat *that*, please?   ____

5 OK, so *that* means we won't be finished before 11 a.m.   ____

6 *That* gives us the average revenue.   ____

2 ◀ᴾ3.02 **Listen and check. Then listen again and practise saying the sentences.**

Unit 4

4.1 Stress in word building

1 Write the words in the correct place in the table, according to their stress pattern.

| analyst   analytical   anticipate   anticipated   anticipation |
| conversion   convert (v)   converted   disruptive   disruptor   innovative |
| innovator   irritable   irritated   irritation   prediction   predictive |

1	oO	
2	Ooo	
3	oOo	
4	Oooo	
5	oOoo	
6	ooOo	
7	oOooo	
8	ooOoo	
9	oooOo	

2 🔊 P4.01 Listen and check. Then listen again and practise saying the words.

4.4 Stress in phrases

1 Each sentence has two stressed words. Before you listen, underline what you think the stressed words will be.

1 Let's think about how to manage this.

2 How could you imagine this working?

3 Tell me about how this situation affects you.

4 What do you think of this?

5 I'll let you know if I'm struggling.

6 Think of some other options to present at the meeting.

7 Get some expert advice before making a decision.

8 Let's try and look at this in the morning.

9 Why don't we approach it from another perspective?

10 It's a great idea, but it's unsatisfactory.

2 🔊 P4.02 Listen and check. Then listen again and practise saying the sentences.

Unit 5

5.2 Intonation and linking words.

1 Underline the linking word(s) in each item.

1 On the one hand, employees have to work more hours, but on the other hand, they receive overtime pay or extra time off.

2 In spite of launching a new and innovative product line, they have lowered their profit expectations.

3 Even though no performance scheme will fit every occasion, the fuel-saving study does suggest an approach worth trying more broadly.

4 Although salaries were not increased for captains, the fact that the company was taking an interest in fuel saving, and acknowledging success, seemed to delight them.

5 Executives are often those who receive performance-related pay. Nevertheless, it is often difficult to evaluate how well they have performed.

6 Despite finding that rewards could lead to employee motivation, management decided to stop the rewards system completely.

7 On the one hand, we keep getting more and more work to do. On the other hand, we were told by management that we shouldn't work overtime.

8 Despite the fact that the targets were set in discussion with department heads, they are proving to be unrealistic in some areas.

9 In spite of the fact that several experiments had shown that it was less effective than other schemes, they continued to use performance-related pay.

2 ◀ P5.01 Listen to the sentences in Exercise 1 and mark the fall–rises.

3 Listen again and practise saying the sentences, using the same intonation as in the recording.

5.3 Intonation when handling challenging feedback

1 ◀ P5.02 Listen to two versions (A and B) of the same response to challenging feedback. Circle the one that is more polite.

1 I'm concerned about the amount of time some members of your team spend around the coffee machine chatting. Coffee is important of course, but we're here to work.

Yes, but you're not seeing the big picture here. Most of the chat is work-related, actually.   A / Ⓑ

2 These figures show that production is at a lower rate than this time last month.

There's room for improvement, I agree, but we've talked about this before.
You have to remember that we predicted this might happen.   A / B

3 There's nowhere for visitors to park because the visitors' car park is full of employees' cars.

Well, I'm not sure what you're saying is necessarily accurate. It's true that a few employees park there because it's more convenient, but 'full' is an exaggeration.   A / B

2 Listen again and repeat the more polite version.

Unit 6

6.2 Contractions and weak forms in third conditionals

1 Before you listen, circle the auxiliary verbs that can be spoken as contracted forms.

1 A: If they had donated even 1 percent of the money they had made to local projects, it would have generated really good publicity for them.

   B: Really? Do you think 1 percent would have been enough?

2 A: Would you have taken the job if they had offered it to you?

   B: Yes, I think I would have.

3 A: How else could we have reduced our costs?

   B: Well, it might have been a good idea to have more virtual meetings.

4 A: Did you consider how much we could have reduced our tax bill if we had given some of our profits to charity?

   B: Yes, it would certainly have been quite a lot.

5 A: They could have cut their carbon emissions considerably if they had had a policy in favour of sourcing materials locally.

   B: Yes, they certainly could have.

6 A: They would not have had such problems with stakeholders if they had not been so secretive about their finances.

   B: No, they certainly would not have.

2 🔊 P6.01 Listen and check.

3 Look at the examples of *have* in Exercise 1. Listen again and underline all weak forms of *have*. There is only one strong form.

4 Listen again and check. Then listen again and practise saying the dialogues.

6.5 Chunking, pausing and stress when reading aloud

1 🔊 P6.02 Listen to someone reading the text aloud and mark the divisions between the chunks.

We encourage all staff to participate in our programme, so you could become a community hero, too. We are currently establishing a project to turn neglected public spaces into useful community gardens where local residents can grow both vegetables and decorative plants. Therefore, if you are interested in gardening or just enjoy working outside, please contact Human Resources immediately.

We are going to run a competition next month so staff can suggest ideas for other projects we can be involved in.

2 Listen again and mark the main stresses. There are one or two per chunk.

3 Practise reading the text aloud.

Unit 7

7.2 Stress and intonation in adverbials and time expressions

1 Write the adverbials and time expressions in the correct place in the table, according to their stress pattern.

| almost never | any day | at the latest | hardly ever | normally | on a daily basis | rarely | seldom |

1	Oo		4	OoOo	
2	Ooo		5	ooOo	
3	OoO		6	ooOoOo	

2 ◀)) P7.01 **Listen and check. Then listen again and practise saying the adverbials and time expressions.**

3 ◀)) P7.02 **Listen and mark the adverbials and time expressions which are stressed and have fall–rise intonation.**

1 Sometimes she works over lunch.

2 Normally I don't work on Fridays.

3 They almost never leave the office before 7 p.m.

4 Many of us sit at our computers all day.

5 From time to time she does administrative work.

6 Usually meetings last about three hours.

7 They put in many hours on a daily basis, but they rarely work at the weekend.

8 You can come by to see me any day.

4 Practise saying the sentences.

5 Cover Exercise 3 and use the prompts below to help you say the sentences from memory.

1 sometimes – lunch

2 normally – Fridays

3 never – office – 7 p.m.

4 us – computers – day

5 time – administrative

6 meetings – three

7 hours – daily – rarely – weekend

8 come – see – any

7.4 Intonation when negotiating

1 ◀)) P7.03 **Listen and repeat.**

1 I know we're both on the same wavelength about their experience.

2 So what you're saying is you definitely won't go?

3 I understand your position, and reluctance, a bit more now.

4 This is a good thing that we can all learn from.

5 In other words, you don't want to send either of them?

2 ◀)) P7.04 **Listen to these poor versions of some sentences. Then try to say them better.**

1 How would you feel if we put you in charge of the project?

2 In your opinion, it should take around a month of local support. Right?

3 We're going to have to go the extra mile to meet the deadline.

4 What that means exactly is that we need to make this a priority.

5 I think we can both agree that we need to develop new workflows.

3 ◀)) P7.05 **Listen and check.**

Unit 8

8.2 /s/, /z/, /ʃ/, /tʃ/ and /dʒ/

1 Look at the words and answer the questions.

> administration application classes clause closed colleagues courageous figures
> graduating necessary once personal process questions special sure technician touch

1 Which word contains both /s/ and /z/? _____

2 Which words contain /ʃ/ once? _____

3 Which words contain /s/ twice? _____

4 Which words contain /dʒ/ once? _____

5 Which word contains /s/, /tʃ/and /z/? _____

6 Which words contain /z/ once? _____

7 Which words contain both /s/ and /ʃ/? _____

8 Which words contain /s/ once? _____

9 Which word contains /tʃ/ once? _____

2 🔊 P8.01 Listen and check.

3 Practise saying the words in Exercise 1.

4 🔊 P8.02 Write the words. Then listen and check.

1 /ʃeəz/ _____ **7** /'sʌbdʒekts/ _____

2 /klɔːz/ _____ **8** /'kɒliːgz/ _____

3 /əd'vaɪs/ _____ **9** /ləʊ'keɪʃn/ _____

4 /əd'vaɪz/ _____ **10** /træn'zɪʃn/ _____

5 /'pæʃən/ _____ **11** /kə'reɪdʒəs/ _____

6 /'mɔːgɪdʒ/ _____ **12** /tek'nɒlədʒɪz/ _____

8.4 Voice range

1 🔊 P8.03 Listen and mark the breaks between the chunks.

Brainstorming generates ideas which other methods do not, due to the freedom it gives people to think creatively. There are no 'golden rules' as such, but these eight stages can definitely help you to have successful stages:

1 Define the goal or desired outcome and the amount of time available.

2 Start with a question or selection of questions.

3 Collect as many ideas as possible, without evaluating them or commenting other than to thank each person for their ideas.

4 Put all of the ideas somewhere everyone can see them, for example, on a board. Then you all decide how to group the ideas.

5 Ask people to give more details about their ideas before evaluating any of them.

6 Only at this point should you start to discuss, evaluate and build on the ideas.

7 Always end with some clear decisions and action points.

And finally,

8 Thank everyone for participating. Even if some individuals didn't come up with the final idea, their presence helped to create the atmosphere that led to the outcome.

2 Listen again and underline the main stress with falling intonation in each chunk.

Answer key

Unit 1

Vocabulary
1
1 structure
2 strategy
3 open-plan
4 atmosphere
5 image
6 flexibility
7 hierarchy
8 values
9 Organisational

2
1 atmosphere
2 dress code
3 some flexibility
4 open-plan
5 minimum salary
6 pay rate

Grammar
1
1 i Future Continuous
   ii Future Perfect Simple

2
1 will be entertaining
2 will be staying
3 Will you have finished
4 will be preparing
5 Will you be sleeping
6 won't have changed
7 will have transferred
8 will be retaining

In progress: 1, 2, 4, 5, 8
Finished: 3, 6, 7

3
1 'll / will be doing
2 'll / will be running
3 'll / will have set up
4 'll / will have finished
5 'll / will be working
6 will you be doing
7 won't have given up
8 'll / will still be going
9 'll / will be travelling
10 'll / will be earning
11 you'll / will still be living
12 'll / will have moved out
13 'll / will be living
14 'll / will be working

Listening
1 1 f 2 a 3 d 4 c
2 1 d 2 a 3 c 4 a
   5 c 6 d
3 1 T
2 F – Although salary was mentioned, a *large* salary was not mentioned as an important factor. *Strong management* was not mentioned.

Functional language
1
1 To be honest, I feel
2 I can see you're concerned
3 we both want to
4 Could we help you
5 One way to solve this is
6 how do you think we can
7 I understand what you're saying
8 Would it be useful
9 let's wait until

2
1 based
2 used to
3 responsible for
4 quite
5 great
6 with
7 on
8 proud to
9 involved
10 need
11 way
12 hesitate

Writing
1A
1 Title
2 Introducing
3 Informing
4 Informing
5 Informing
6 Informing
7 Concluding

B Section 2 ... the company **is** happy to ...
Section 3 ... the opportunity **to** study ...
Section 4 ... so you **are** sure to find ...
Section 5 ... this will **be** reimbursed...
Section 6 ... appreciate you **are** likely ...
Section 7 ... do not hesitate **to** contact us ...

2 Model answer
STOP PRESS: opportunity to work abroad for three months!
Why not take advantage of our work abroad programme? The company is happy to announce we are offering employees the opportunity to work abroad for three months in one of our international offices, including Mexico City, Vancouver and Shanghai. The aim of the programme is to encourage effective collaboration and build trust between our international offices. The temporary job positions on offer are at different times during the year, summer or winter, and your accommodation will be paid for by the company.
Please note that successful applicants will be staying with a host family in order to help you adapt to the country and learn the local language. Let us know if you wish to participate in our 'work exchange' programme. We appreciate you are likely to have concerns about working abroad or your choice of location. The HR department is happy to answer any questions you may have. Click on the link below to find out more. Please don't hesitate to contact us for more information.

3 Option c is the best option: *Don't hesitate to contact us or click on the link below to find out more about this exciting programme.* This is because it invites the reader to do one of two things: contact the company or click on the link for more information. This is called 'a call to action' – what you want the reader to do.
Option a doesn't tell the reader how to contact the company.
Option b only tells the reader to click on the link but doesn't explain why, so the reader may or may not click on the link.

Unit 2

Vocabulary
1
1 induction programme
2 mentees
3 online courses
4 blended learning
5 job-related
6 career development

2
1 analytical 2 competency
3 intelligence 4 learner
5 mentee 6 mentoring
7 motivation 8 motivated
9 trainer 10 train

3
1 needs analysis
2 understanding
3 training courses
4 skills set
5 emotional
6 benchmarking
7 standard
8 learning

Grammar
1
1 should be trained
2 needs to be improved
3 must be held
4 can't be offered
5 doesn't have to be done
6 shouldn't be taught
7 have to be given
8 has to be decided, should be taught

2 1 b 2 d 3 a 4 b 5 d 6 c

Reading
1
1 Designing career development programmes
2 Report writing
3 Designing online learning platforms
4 Motivating staff: communicating with remote teams
5 Health and safety: training your guard dog
6 Mindfulness: dealing with stress
7 Communication skills and conflict resolution
8 Repairing buses or trains

2
1 face-to-face
2 job-oriented
3 online learning
4 job-oriented
5 blended learning
6 career development
7 face-to-face
8 career development
9 blended learning
10 job-oriented
11 face-to-face
12 job-oriented
13 online learning

3
1 Motivating staff: communicating with remote teams
2 Communication skills and conflict resolution
3 Mindfulness: dealing with stress
4 Report writing

Functional language

1 1 a 2 c 3 c 4 b 5 a

2A 1 What we're looking to do here today
2 it's important for everyone
3 I want to come to that
4 and then discuss
5 So, just to recap
6 we have made good progress
7 I'm afraid time is pressing

B b

Writing

1A a believe b attached
c motivate d appreciate
e possible f interested
g helpful h attend

B Requests: 1, 3, 5, 9

Reasons: 2, 4, 6, 7, 8

2 Model answer
Dear HR Manager,
I am writing to request some training in designing online learning platforms because I have been asked to be part of a team that is currently designing a new platform for our organisation. I have some basic knowledge of online learning platforms, but it would be extremely helpful for me to learn more.
I would, therefore, like to request the Intermediate blended learning course of sixty hours. I would appreciate it if you let me know by the end of the week as I see that the evening face-to-face course starts next week. I am afraid I am unable to do the morning one because of my work commitments. It would be very helpful for me to do this course as my team hopes to improve the training and development of all our employees. Please see attached my application form. I look forward to hearing from you soon.
Kind regards,
Biyu Wu

Unit 3

Vocabulary

1 Across:
3 recession 4 loans 6 savings
8 investment 9 bankruptcy
Down:
1 mortgage 2 depression
4 losses 5 crunch 7 stock

2 1 drop 2 bankrupt 3 lend
4 recover 5 booming 6 bailed

3 1 crash 2 rating 3 downturn
4 economy 5 institutions
6 devastating

Grammar

1 1 's / is likely that
2 're / are likely to
3 's / is due to
4 's / is unlikely that
5 're / are unlikely to
6 probably

2 1 will definitely be a success
2 It's / It is probable that
3 They're / They are due to
4 It's / It is improbable that
5 's / is unlikely to be as successful
6 We'll / We will probably

3 1 We will **probably** reach our sales target this quarter.
2 They're on schedule, and they're **also** going to meet their budget.
3 Their profits are **likely** to increase next year.
4 We're **unlikely** to make a loss.
5 They **probably** won't accept the proposed terms of the sponsorship deal.
6 Do they **also** hope to increase online sales?

Listening

1 1 F 2 T 3 F 4 T 5 T 6 F
7 T 8 T

2 1 it's likely that
2 is certain
3 is going to
4 it's probable that
5 also plans
6 will probably
7 is unlikely
8 is likely to

3 b

Functional language

1 1 a 2 b 3 a 4 a 5 b 6 b

2 1 clarify, following
2 confirm, double-check
3 specifically
4 remind
5 went
6 saying
7 I understood you correctly

Writing

1 1 economy 2 margins
3 quarter 4 revenue 5 posted
6 flow 7 invested 8 debt
9 dividend 10 forecast

2 1 Overview/Introduction
2 Reasons for performance
3 Positive aspects
4 Negative aspects
5 Future outlook

3 Model answer
The last year has seen the company making great progress, in spite of the economic downturn in Asia. This was largely as a result of a decrease in the cost of materials. This meant that we finished more strongly than expected in the final quarter with growth of 3% on the previous quarter.
The start of the year gave us cause to be optimistic. Sales revenue in the first quarter was up 3% from the previous quarter. However, in the second and third quarters, our sales volume dropped by 2%. For the year, we posted sales of €98 million, down 2% on the previous year. Cash flow from operations was €52 million and we invested €3 million in capital expenditure including a new fleet of delivery vehicles. We also repaid €3.5 million of debt which we had borrowed for our new offices. Despite our drop in sales, we were able to hold our annual dividend at €2.30. Last year, we launched a completely new website, and customers love it. Fortunately, the forecast for the coming year looks promising.

4 c

Unit 4

Vocabulary

1 1 c 2 a 3 b 4 c 5 a 6 b

2 1 convert 2 personalisation
3 irritating 4 analyse
5 prediction 6 visual

3 1 Disruptive 2 innovation
3 anticipate 4 predicted
5 disruption 6 irritation
7 analysts

Grammar

1 1 hate, have 2 is, travel
3 won't, change 4 If, you'll
5 lost, wouldn't 6 would, had

2 1 b 2 a 3 b 4 a 5 b 6 a

3 1 Provided 2 Unless 3 as long
4 condition 5 if

Reading

1 1 c 2 a 3 e

2 1 T 2 F 3 T 4 F 5 F 6 T
7 T 8 F

3 b

Functional language

1 1 I'd like to stick to our agenda
2 That's really outside the scope of this meeting
3 We do need to deal with production costs

4 We can come back to it
5 Let her finish her point
6 Can we slow down a little?
2 **1** a **2** g **3** d **4** i **5** c **6** h
7 e **8** f **9** b

Writing

1 **1** propose **2** complaints
3 ease **4** solution **5** prefer
6 initial **7** recover
8 recommend

2A **1** Introduction or purpose statement
2 Brief summary of problem
3 Solution to problem
4 Plan, costs and schedule
5 Conclusion

B b–The notes mention that some customers may not be confident about pronouncing unfamiliar food names, and that the menu could be provided in several languages.

3 **Model answer**
Automated Restaurant Order Kiosk Proposal
I propose that we invest in an automated ordering system for the hotel restaurant. Recently, there have been more complaints about waiting times during the busy periods of 7.30–8.30 a.m. and 1.00–2.00 p.m., and food quality in the restaurant. However, our long-term strategy is to reduce customer waiting time and to modernise the restaurant experience.
Five automated ordering kiosks would be an excellent solution. Most customers like to see pictures of the food, and this would provide that. And for people who prefer to order in their own language, the kiosks could provide the menu in several languages. Research shows that kiosk ordering reduces stress for customers who aren't confident pronouncing the names of unfamiliar foods.
Installing two kiosks first would be a good way for us to measure customer preferences. Although initial investment would be relatively high, in the long run, kiosks are cheaper than employing waiting staff. Five ordering kiosks could replace three waiters. This would give us an overall saving which would allow us to improve the quality of our food.
In conclusion, I therefore recommend we invest in two automated ordering kiosks immediately and plan to order three more before the end of the year.

Unit 5

Vocabulary

1 **1** succeed
2 appraisal
3 failed
4 promotion
5 failure
6 promoted
7 achievements
8 success

2 **1** failure
2 evaluate
3 promotion
4 reward
5 success
6 recognition
7 appraisal

Grammar

1 **1** b **2** a **3** c **4** d **5** d **6** a
7 b **8** c

2 **1** g **2** h **3** f **4** a **5** e **6** d
7 b **8** c

Listening

1 **1** F **2** T **3** F **4** F **5** T **6** T
7 T **8** T **9** T **10** F

2 **1** However **2** although
3 on the other hand **4** although
5 though **6** despite

3 **1** a **2** a **3** b

4 b

Functional language

1 Defending a position: 1b, 2a, 3a, 4a, 5b
Accepting criticism: 1a, 2b, 3b, 4b, 5a

2 **1** c **2** a **3** d **4** b **5** e
6 g **7** f

Writing

1 **1** I am pleased to report that
2 You demonstrate the ability to
3 In addition, you exhibit the skill to
4 I am impressed by your work so far
5 You show a great aptitude for
6 However, I feel that you need to
7 Although your
8 you always meet the deadlines for
9 Nevertheless, I am confident that
10 Keep up

2 **1** CC **2** PC **3** CC **4** PC **5** CC
6 PC **7** PC **8** CC

3 **Model answer**
I am very pleased with your achievements over the year, and particularly with the fact that our latest project was completed on schedule and within budget. You have displayed considerable communication and team-working skills. The feedback from your line manager and the other team

members praises you for listening actively and giving clear advice whenever it is needed.
In addition, you show a great aptitude for learning advanced computer skills.
Overall, your organisational skills are good. Nevertheless, you should try to prioritise your tasks, not only on a given day, but also over a week. This will make it easier for you at times when you have to work under pressure. In addition, I have also noticed that you are not always able to attend meetings regularly, most probably because there are sometimes too many demands on your time. This can easily be resolved by talking to your line manager a few days in advance. Keep up the good work!

Unit 6

Vocabulary

1 **1** ethical **2** designer **3** show
4 retailer **5** industry

2 **1** clothing brands
2 unethical conduct
3 fair-trade cotton
4 moral approach
5 low pay
6 environmental impact
7 ethically sourced
8 tough conditions

3 **1** across **2** conditions
3 against **4** aware **5** on
6 of **7** for

Grammar

1 **1** could have advertised
2 hadn't paid
3 Would you have had
4 had recycled
5 would have
6 hadn't given

2 **1** hadn't / had not been
2 'd / had had
3 would've / would have paid
4 would've / would have been
5 had grown **6** 'd / had cycled

3 **1** had paid, wouldn't have got
2 wouldn't have had, hadn't made
3 hadn't given, wouldn't have been
4 hadn't presented, wouldn't have gone
5 would have got, had reduced

Reading

1 **1** d **2** a **3** c **4** b **5** f **6** e
7 h **8** g

2 **1** the Netherlands
2 ethical
3 criminals
4 organic
5 environmental damage
6 through cooperation

3 b

Functional language

1
1 I'm afraid 2 concerned
3 I'm not entirely sure
4 To be honest
5 It's just a thought

2 1 b 2 g 3 c 4 a 5 e 6 h
7 d 8 f

Writing

1
1 As
2 Therefore
3 so
4 that

2 1 b, e
2 d, f
3 a, c

3 **Model answer**
Educational Outreach Success
As part of our 'Good Neighbour' programme, our Education Outreach team has met with representatives from three local high schools and have offered financial help with university expenses for bright students who might struggle to pay for college. At a recent presentation, CEO Joelle Van Espen said, 'If I hadn't had the opportunity to go university, I would never have started this company. We need to support education.'
This month, we're scheduling more meetings with school heads. We're currently looking for volunteers to visit schools and talk to students about the programme, and to explain the application process. At the same time, we're trying to make them aware of the work we do here, and the career possibilities we offer.
The Education Outreach project has been so successful so far that we're going to set up a work experience programme for local high-school students. This will allow local students to get valuable work experience, and it will also allow us to identify students who could offer a great benefit to the company as employees in the future. If you don't take this brilliant opportunity to give something back to the young people of the community, then someone else will. Olivia in Human Resources will answer any questions you have, and take the names of volunteers.

4 c

Unit 7

Vocabulary

1 1 set 2 identify 3 schedule
4 allocate 5 maximise 6 use
7 measure 8 take

2
1 on time
2 out of time
3 at a time
4 at the same time
5 ahead of time
6 by the time

3 1 c 2 a 3 f 4 b 5 e 6 d

Grammar

1 1 always 2 usually / frequently
3 frequently / usually 4 now and then 5 sometimes / rarely / seldom 6 seldom / rarely / sometimes 7 rarely / seldom / sometimes 8 hardly ever
9 never

2 1 f 2 b 3 c 4 a 5 d 6 e

3 1 Occasionally
2 never
3 At first, I didn't like
4 She's always
5 normally work
6 going home in a few hours
7 I hardly ever
8 customers now and then
9 I'm rarely
10 From time to time he's

Listening

1 1 now and then 2 never
3 recently 4 rarely 5 often
6 never 7 rarely 8 frequently

2 1 c 2 a 3 d 4 b 5 c 6 a
7 c 8 d

3 b – Speaker 1
c – Speaker 4

Functional language

1 1 f 2 a 3 b 4 d 5 c 6 e

2A 1 b 2 a 3 c 4 a 5 c

B a 2a b 4a c 5c d 3c e 1b

Writing

1 1 problem 2 deadline
3 reason 4 due 5 propose
6 solve 7 reassess
8 inconvenience

2 1 a 2 b 3 a

3 1 Reasons
2 Actions
3 Problems

4 **Model answer**
I'm really sorry to tell you that we've hit a big problem with the new office security system. Consequently, I don't think we'll be able to meet the deadline set for the installation. The main reason for this is that the supplier is unable to deliver all thirty of the security cameras we need. In addition, there is a problem using the current employee ID cards with the new door system due to an update in the manufacturer's electronic locks. We're currently looking at alternatives.
The supplier can deliver twenty cameras now and has promised to send the other ten by the end of next week. I propose that we install the twenty we have now and re-schedule part of the work until we have the additional ten cameras. We may need to reconsider the electronic door locks, or we may also need to replace all employees' ID cards. The delay is going to have a knock-on effect for the security system going live. I apologise for the inconvenience caused and promise to sort it out as soon as possible. I'll keep you updated at all times.

Unit 8

Vocabulary

1 1 keep growing 2 to move
3 weigh up 4 communicate
5 the move 6 efficient

2 1 teamwork 2 cope 3 risk
4 apprehensive 5 consult
6 benefit
Hidden word: morale

3 1 successful 2 plan 3 engaged
4 risk 5 improve 6 benefits
7 implemented 8 adaptable

Grammar

1 1 told 2 had studied 3 her
4 had been 5 liked 6 told
7 was going to have to find
8 were 9 said
10 had supported

2 1 promised 2 suggested
3 confirmed 4 complained
5 informed 6 advised

3 1 a 2 b 3 b 4 a 5 b

Reading

1 1 b 2 e 3 a 4 c 5 f 6 d

2 1 Heinz 2 Maria 3 Mandy
4 Mandy 5 Heinz 6 Maria

3 b – 'This is the time when you need to address any worries that people might have about the change'; Heinz complained that change is never easy.
c – 'Once people are used to the new way of doing things, it's a good time to reflect on what has actually changed. Compare your actual results with what you imagined at the beginning.'; 'I always learn from the things that didn't go as planned.'
e – '… make sure that you can clearly explain to yourself why the change will be a real improvement'; Heinz complained that change is never easy; 'I assure you – things rarely go perfectly, so you will need to identify and solve any problems that have

arisen. As people start to get used to a new way of doing things, everyone has to make sure they don't return to old habits. Continue to focus on the benefits of the change.'

Functional language

1 1 a 2 b 3 b 4 a 5 b
6 a 7 a

2 1 c 2 h 3 a 4 g 5 b 6 e
7 f 8 d

Writing

1 1 announced 2 informed
3 regretted 4 expected
5 assured 6 promised

2 1 News and key facts 2 Further details 3 Quotation and apology
4 Future promises

3 **Model answer**
Mobile phone maker SmaHan has announced plans to close their research and development centre near Mumbai by the end of this week. The centre, which first opened two years ago, came up with the design for SmaHan's most recent model, the SH-X, which performed below expectations in the market.

The management team and engineers at the centre have been informed of the decision and redundancy packages agreed. SmaHan will pay for the rental property until the lease ends in three months, unless they can find someone to take over.

SmaHan is determined to continue offering low-price, fashionable smartphones and intends to learn from the mistakes made in producing the SH-X. CEO Jinsoo Park said he regretted the closure, which was partly caused by his own failure to choose the development team carefully enough. He insisted that all of the engineers at the facility were very talented, but that the company failed to help them understand its vision clearly.

It's expected that none of the Mumbai-based team will return to the office. Mr Park assured SmaHan SH-X owners that the company will continue to support the product, and promised to issue software updates in the near future that would solve some of the problems that users are complaining about.

Pronunciation

Unit 1

1.1

1 Stress on the first word:
car loan
card payment
credit card debt
dress code
fund transfers
job application
pay structure
working atmosphere

Stress on the second word:
company practices
customer support representative
minimum salary

1.2

1
1 By the middle of the next century, workplace culture will have changed drastically.
2 We hope our employees care whether or not <u>we will</u> be making a profit in the future as our success depends on it.
3 Within a few years, these new initiatives will have made a real difference.
4 My company just announced that next year <u>they will</u> be changing the dress code to business casual.
5 There's a lot of discussion about what companies will be doing in the future to keep their employees motivated.
6 The Managing Board has announced that in order to retain young staff members, <u>they will</u> have implemented a scheme for swifter promotions by the beginning of next year.

2
1 By the middle of the next century, workplace culture will have changed drastically.
2 We hope our employees care whether or not we <u>will</u> be making a profit in the future as our success depends on it.
3 Within a few years, these new initiatives will have made a real difference.
4 My company just announced that next month they <u>will</u> be changing the dress code to business casual.
5 There's a lot of discussion about what companies will be doing in the future to keep their employees motivated.
6 The Managing Board has announced that in order to retain young staff members, they <u>will</u> have implemented a scheme for swifter promotions by the beginning of next year.

3
1 By the middle of the next century, workplace culture will <u>have</u> changed drastically.
2 Within a few years, these new initiatives will <u>have</u> made a real difference.
3 The Managing Board has announced that in order to retain young staff members, they will <u>have</u> implemented a scheme for swifter promotions by the beginning of next year.

Unit 2

2.1

1
1 **a** the mentor
   b act, guide, offer support
2 **a** training, development
   b critical
3 **a** learn, adapt
   b because, constantly changing

2.4

1

/v/	/w/
of a	to express
have a	to each
effective if	
/r/	
their ideas	
are often	
more effective	
share responsibility	

Unit 3

3.3

1
1 c
2 d
3 a
4 b
5 d

3.4

1
1 *W*
2 *W*
3 *S*
4 *W*
5 *S*
6 *S*

Unit 4

4.1

1

1	oO	convert
2	Ooo	analyst
3	oOo	conversion converted disruptive disruptor prediction predictive
4	Oooo	innovator innovative irritable irritated
5	oOoo	anticipate
6	ooOo	irritation
7	oOooo	anticipated
8	ooOoo	analytical
9	oooOo	anticipation

4.4

2
1 Let's think about how to <u>manage</u> this.
2 <u>How</u> could you imagine this <u>working</u>?
3 <u>Tell</u> me about how this situation <u>affects</u> you.
4 <u>What</u> do you think of <u>this</u>?
5 I'll <u>let</u> you know if I'm <u>struggling</u>.
6 <u>Think</u> of some <u>other</u> options to present at the meeting.
7 Get some expert advice <u>before</u> making a <u>decision</u>.
8 <u>Let's</u> try and <u>look</u> at this in the morning.
9 Why don't we approach it from <u>another perspective</u>?
10 It's a <u>great</u> idea, but it's <u>unsatisfactory</u>.

Unit 5

5.2

1
1 <u>On the one hand</u>, employees have to work more hours, but <u>on the other hand</u>, they receive overtime pay or extra time off.
2 <u>In spite of</u> launching a new and innovative product line, they have lowered their profit expectations.
3 <u>Even though</u> no performance scheme will fit every occasion, the fuel-saving study does suggest an approach worth trying more broadly.
4 <u>Although</u> salaries were not increased for captains, the fact that the company was taking an interest in fuel saving, and acknowledging success, seemed to delight them.
5 Executives are often those who receive performance-related pay. <u>Nevertheless</u>, it is often difficult to evaluate how well they have performed.
6 <u>Despite</u> finding that rewards could lead to employee motivation, management decided to stop the rewards system completely.
7 <u>On the one hand</u>, we keep getting more and more work to do. <u>On the other hand</u>, we were told by management that we shouldn't work overtime.
8 <u>Despite the fact that</u> the targets were set in discussion with department heads, they are proving to be unrealistic in some areas.
9 <u>In spite of the fact that</u> several experiments had shown that it was less effective than other schemes, they continued to use performance-related pay.
10 We have looked into faster advancement for young people. <u>However</u>, it is not always possible to set a policy which is fair for all.

2 **1** On the <u>one hand</u>, employees have to work more hours, but on the <u>other hand</u>, they receive overtime pay or extra time off.
2 In spite of launching a new and innovative <u>product line</u>, they have lowered their profit expectations.
3 Even though no performance scheme will fit <u>every occasion</u>, the fuel-saving study does suggest an approach worth trying more broadly.
4 Although salaries were not <u>increased for captains</u>, the fact that the company was taking an interest in fuel saving, and acknowledging success, seemed to delight them.
5 Executives are often those who receive performance-related pay. <u>Nevertheless</u>, it is often difficult to evaluate how well they have performed.
6 Despite finding that rewards could lead to employee <u>motivation</u>, management decided to stop the rewards system completely.
7 On the <u>one hand</u>, we keep getting more and more work to do. On the <u>other hand</u>, we were told by management that we shouldn't work overtime.
8 Despite the fact that the targets were set in discussion with <u>department heads</u>, they are proving to be unrealistic in some areas.
9 In spite of the fact that several experiments had shown that it was less effective than <u>other schemes</u>, they continued to use performance-related pay.

5.3
1 **1** B
2 B
3 B

Unit 6

6.2
2 **1** A: If they had donated even 1 percent of the money they had made to local projects, it would have generated really good publicity for them.
B: Really? Do you think 1 percent would have been enough?
2 A: Would you have taken the job if they had offered it to you?
B: Yes, I think I would have.
3 A: How else could we have reduced our costs?
B: Well, it might have been a good idea to have more virtual meetings.

4 A: Did you consider how much we could have reduced our tax bill if we had given some of our profits to charity?
B: Yes, it would certainly have been quite a lot.
5 A: They could have cut their carbon emissions considerably if they had had a policy in favour of sourcing materials locally.
B: Yes, they certainly could have.
6 A: They would not have had such problems with stakeholders if they had not been so secretive about their finances.
B: No, they certainly would not have.

4 **1** A: If they'd donated even 1 percent of the money they'd made to local projects, it would <u>have</u> generated really good publicity for them.
B: Really? Do you think 1 percent would <u>have</u> been enough?
2 A: Would you <u>have</u> taken the job if they'd offered it to you?
B: Yes, I think I would <u>have</u>.
3 A: How else could we <u>have</u> reduced our costs?
B: Well, it might <u>have</u> been a good idea to have (strong form) more virtual meetings.
4 A: Did you consider how much we could <u>have</u> reduced our tax bill if we'd given some of our profits to charity?
B: Yes, it would certainly <u>have</u> been quite a lot.
5 A: They could <u>have</u> cut their carbon emissions considerably if they'd had a policy in favour of sourcing materials locally.
B: Yes, they certainly could <u>have</u>.
6 A: They wouldn't <u>have</u> had such problems with stakeholders if they hadn't been so secretive about their finances.
B: No, they certainly wouldn't <u>have</u>.

6.5
1 We encourage all staff | to participate in our programme, | so you could become a community hero, too. | We are currently establishing a project | to turn neglected public spaces | into useful community gardens | where local residents | can grow both vegetables | and decorative plants. | Therefore, | if you are interested in gardening | or just enjoy working outside, | please contact Human Resources immediately.
We are going to run a competition next month | so staff can suggest ideas for other projects we can be involved in. | A fabulous holiday | is the prize for the winning idea.

2 We encourage <u>all</u> staff | to par<u>ti</u>cipate in our <u>programme</u>, | so <u>you</u> could become a community hero, <u>too</u>. | We are <u>currently</u> establishing a <u>project</u> | to turn ne<u>glec</u>ted public <u>spaces</u> | into <u>useful</u> community <u>gardens</u> | where <u>local residents</u> | can <u>grow</u> both <u>vegetables</u> | and <u>decorative plants</u>. | Therefore, | if <u>you</u> are interested in <u>gardening</u> | or just enjoy <u>working</u> outside, | <u>please</u> contact Human Resources im<u>me</u>diately.
We are <u>going</u> to run a compe<u>ti</u>tion next month | so <u>staff</u> can suggest ideas for <u>other</u> projects we can be involved in.

Unit 7

7.2
1

1	Oo	rarely, seldom
2	Ooo	normally
3	OoO	any day
4	OoOo	almost never, hardly ever
5	ooOo	at the latest
6	ooOoOo	on a daily basis

3 **1** <u>Sometimes</u> she works over lunch.
2 <u>Normally</u> I don't work on Fridays.
3 They almost never leave the office before 7 p.m.
4 Many of us sit at our computers all day.
5 <u>From time to time</u> she does administrative work.
6 <u>Usually</u> meetings last about three hours.
7 They put in many hours on a daily basis, but they rarely work at the weekend.
8 You can come by to see me <u>any day</u>.

Unit 8

8.2
1 **1** classes
2 application, sure, technician
3 necessary, process
4 courageous, graduating
5 questions
6 clause, closed, colleagues, figures
7 administration, special
8 once, personal
9 touch

4 **1** shares **2** clause **3** advice
4 advise **5** passion
6 mortgage **7** subjects
8 colleagues **9** location
10 transition **11** courageous
12 technologies

8.4

1 Brainstorming generates ideas which other methods do not, | due to the freedom it gives people to think creatively. | There are no 'golden rules' as such, | but these eight stages can definitely help you to have successful stages: |
1 | Define the goal or desired outcome | and the amount of time available. |
2 | Start with a question | or selection of questions. |
3 | Collect as many ideas as possible, | without evaluating them or commenting | other than to thank each person for their ideas. |
4 | Put all of the ideas somewhere everyone can see them, | for example, on a board. | Then you all decide, how to group the ideas. |
5 | Ask people to give more details about their ideas | before evaluating any of them. |
6 | Only at this point | should you start to discuss, evaluate and build on the ideas. |
7 | Always end with some clear decisions | and action points. | And finally, |
8 | Thank everyone for participating. | Even if some individuals didn't come up with the final idea, | their presence helped to create the atmosphere that led to the outcome.

8 | Thank everyone for participating. | Even if some individuals didn't come up with the final idea, | their presence helped to create the atmosphere that led to the outcome.

2 Brainstorming generates ideas which other methods do not, | due to the freedom it gives people to think creatively. | There are no 'golden rules' as such, | but these eight stages can definitely help you to have successful stages: |
1 | Define the goal or desired outcome | and the amount of time available. |
2 | Start with a question | or selection of questions. |
3 | Collect as many ideas as possible, | without evaluating them or commenting | other than to thank each person for their ideas. |
4 | Put all of the ideas somewhere everyone can see them, | for example, on a board. | Then you all decide how to group the ideas. |
5 | Ask people to give more details about their ideas | before evaluating any of them. |
6 | Only at this point | should you start to discuss, evaluate and build on the ideas. |
7 | Always end with some clear decisions | and action points. | And finally,

Audioscripts

1.01

I = Interviewer **E** = Expert

I: So, Katherine, what motivates us at work? What are the factors that affect a young person when they're deciding where they'd like to work?

E: Well, what motivates us can depend on many things but the happiness of employees is something that has been given more importance in recent years. It isn't just about the salary. The pay rate is important but it isn't the only motivational factor that concerns millennials, or the 'Y' generation. To give one example, a younger colleague recently complained to me that our company kitchen only had cow's milk. She told me her previous employer had offered both soya and rice milk! Little things can make a difference and help to create a good working environment.

I: Wow! Soya milk? But what about younger people's attitude to corporate culture?

E: When it comes to company culture, millennials often prefer a more casual dress code compared to their older colleagues who will be wearing a style that's more business casual. Younger employees also really enjoy doing fun team-building activities to get to know each other, both at work and outside work. On the other hand, those with young children, will appreciate having flexibility in their work schedule and the chance of working from home a couple of days a week. And they obviously won't be socialising so much after working hours.

I: Are there any other key factors when a young person is deciding which job to take?

E: I'd say a company's principles and beliefs is a decisive factor when accepting a job offer. Most people want to work for a company where they share the same values as their colleagues. Another key factor is having shared goals: for example, wanting to reach your team's monthly sales targets, or wanting to deliver a quality service to clients.

I: And is it a good idea to involve all staff in strategy planning? Or should that be left to management?

E: Asking employees what they think when developing company strategy can make all employees feel more valued and motivated. It's the best way to get staff members to care about the company's future. This type of motivation helps to retain staff and encourages growth. Finally, whatever the organisational behaviour, any successful organisation needs a structure where there are opportunities for promotion and personal development as well as a recruitment strategy for attracting the right kind of employee who will work well with the rest of the staff and contribute to its continued success.

1.02

D = Dominique **K** = Karl

D: As I mentioned in our last call, Karl, I think quality is becoming a concern on this project. To be honest, I feel a little worried about delivering a quality product to the customer.

K: Really? I can see you're concerned about quality but I thought you were happy that we had managed to reduce costs.

D: Yes, we both want to keep to budget, but frankly I'm concerned that we're losing quality and our customers won't buy the software. Could we help you to test quality more effectively in some way?

K: Well, until now we've only tested the software using a small number of people. One way to solve this is to test it using another group with very different needs, but we don't have a budget for that.

D: I like your suggestion, Karl, and I realise testing is expensive. Based on your experience, how do you think we can test the software without increasing the budget too much? Could we reduce the number of people in the first group, and then create a second group for testing?

K: I understand what you're saying but it's important to have at least twelve people in each group and currently we have one group of eighteen testers.

D: Would it be useful for us to create another group of twelve testers but reduce the first group from eighteen to twelve? That would mean paying for only six more testers.

K: Sure. That could work. But let's wait until we have the test results from this week and then decide together. And we need to make sure the second group have different software requirements.

D: Thanks, Karl. I knew we could come up with something.

1.03

Hello. My name's Lotte Smit and I'm based in the Tokyo office. I've been with this company for around two years. We work on engineering projects. I'm a key account manager. In the past I used to work in Europe, but since last year I've been working on projects in South-East Asia as I'm now responsible for key accounts in Japan and Australia. What else? Well, I have to travel quite a lot; half of my time is travelling around Japan, Australia and New Zealand. The job is quite stressful but I really enjoy it. And I have to say, it's going to be great working with you on this project and I'm proud to be involved. Finally, if you need my help in any way, don't hesitate to ask. I'm here to collaborate. Thank you.

2.01

C = Carrie **T** = Thom **V** = Valeria

C: Good morning, everyone. Thank you for joining us on this call. What we're looking to do here today is to choose the best digital learning platform. First we'll hear from Valeria from IT. Then, as we discuss things, it's important for everyone to contribute their ideas.

T: Hi Carrie, Thom here in Berlin. Can we talk about budget as I think this has a massive impact on the way we digitalise everything?

C: Oh, sorry, Thom, I want to come to that later but can we just go around the table first and then discuss? Valeria has been working on ideas for the digital learning platform with her team. Let's begin with you, Valeria. Can you kick us off?

V: Thanks Carrie. First, I'd like to share my screen. As you can see on your screens, the digital platform needs to offer different types of training programmes, including blended learning, and practical courses for...

T: Sorry, can I stop you there? Valeria, I can't see the platform.

C: OK, Thom, bear with us. Can you share the screen with Thom, please?

V: Yeah, sure. Give me a minute...

C: That's great, Valeria. So, just to recap everything, we all agree to offer more online courses, and some blended learning, and Thom thinks that the digital platform will definitely reduce trainings costs. I think we have made good progress here today. Perhaps the next step would be to look at the risks when digitalising learning, especially for certain skills courses that we usually do face-to-face. It is definitely important, but I'm afraid time is pressing, so we'll need to discuss this in our next call. Valeria, you'll send us some screenshots of how it will work. And I'll email round the summary of today's meeting. Thanks everyone!

V & T: Bye / Speak soon / Thanks Carrie.

🔊 3.01

French carmaker Renault has announced plans to increase profitability and double sales outside of Europe in the next five years. The company hopes to increase its market share in Africa, India and Brazil, and also to reduce production costs by one billion euros. As a result of the announcement, Renault shares are up by 1.48 percent. Analysts say it's likely that the trend will continue.

Renault and Japanese carmakers Nissan and Mitsubishi have said that their strategic partnership alliance is certain to become more like a single company, with the aim of sharing more technology and manufacturing facilities. The businesses hope to spread the costs of product development.

Chief Executive Carlos Ghosn says that while the company was more concerned with recovery in previous quarters, they're now focussing on profitability. As part of its five-year plan, Renault is going to launch eight new electric cars. This is likely to become increasingly important in the next few years, as it's probable that petrol cars will be banned in many markets by 2040.

In addition to promoting low-priced cars in Brazil and India, the company plans to launch seven new cars in China. Renault also wants to increase growth in Iran and Russia, as well as North Africa.

Renault's Spanish rival SEAT, which became profitable last year after ten years of losses, is also preparing for international expansion. The company hopes to use its Spanish heritage to connect with car buyers in Central and South America. Chief Executive Luca de Meo thinks the company, which currently sells ninety percent of its cars in Europe, will probably make a third of its sales outside of Europe ten years from now. SEAT's more immediate goal is to attract young people to its brand by offering inexpensive vehicles. The challenge of this approach, according to Mr de Meo, is that while young people want cheap transport, they don't necessarily want to own a car. He has suggested that the business may need to focus less on selling cars to think more in terms of providing transport services. However, JPMorgan analyst José Asumendi says that SEAT is unlikely to succeed unless the company focuses on car sales, not on breaking into the service market.

In order to boost its appeal with younger drivers, SEAT is going to make its cars technologically connected. The company is likely to launch an app, probably in the next few months, that drivers can use to check how much petrol the car has, and to unlock the doors or operate the air conditioning, even when they're not in the car. SEAT's most recent reported operating profit was €143.5 million, compared with a loss of €7.3 million a year earlier.

🔊 3.02

1 Analysts say it's likely that the increase in Renault's share price will continue.
2 Renault, Nissan and Mitsubishi say that their partnership is certain to become more like a single company.
3 Renault is going to launch eight new electric cars.
4 In many places, it's probable that petrol cars will be banned by 2040.
5 In addition to work in Brazil, India and China, Renault also wants to increase growth in Iran, Russia and North Africa.
6 Ten years from now, SEAT will probably make more than 30 percent of its sales outside Europe.
7 One analyst said that if SEAT tries to break into the service market, it's unlikely to succeed.
8 In the next few months, SEAT is likely to launch an app.

🔊 5.01

B = Boris   **L** = Livia

B: Livia, there's something I want to ask you. I was reading this article about motivating and rewarding employees, and it got me thinking about all sorts of things ... We've been colleagues for a few years, so I hope you don't mind my asking. Tell me, would you work harder if you got a pay rise?

L: You mean, you think I don't work hard enough?

B: Ha ha ha. No, of course not. Let me put it this way: you work hard, we all know that, and you get a fair wage ... However, perhaps a pay rise or a bonus of some sort would motivate you to work even harder ...

L: Well, the thing is, I don't think I could possibly work harder than I've been working over the past three years. I consider myself lucky to have a job that brings me more than a pay cheque at the end of the month. I simply do my best, I find satisfaction in what I do, and really, although not all my projects are very successful, I can't see how I could possibly work better or more. And honestly, I believe that all our colleagues are basically like that.

B: Yeah, so do I. ... You know, the stuff I was reading, sometimes it gave me the impression that it had a rather pessimistic view of human nature ... You know, as if people were naturally lazy ... Just trying to get away with doing the least possible amount of work ...

L: I know what you mean. Some employers unfortunately seem to think that money is the only thing that motivates people ...

B: I know! Financial incentives are important, of course, but on the other hand it would be a very sad world if we only worked to earn a better salary ...

L: ... or if money was the only thing a job had to offer ...

B: Exactly! You know, when I hear my parents talk about their experience of work, there's a word they often use, it's 'solidarity' ...

L: These days you hardly ever hear that word, do you? It's all about productivity, competition, things like that, although what we need most, in my opinion, is to be part of a group with common interests and objectives.

B: That's right ... Employees need a real connection with the workplace, not just an internet connection. We need to interact with other people face to face, not just on the phone. We need a sense of mutual trust with our colleagues and with our managers ... and also to feel that we all have a common goal ...

L: It's a bit like football, isn't it? Like football teams, companies compete with one another, but inside the team, it's all support and solidarity ... To me, getting colleagues to compete with one another is the most horrible form of management ...

B: Yeah ... It's happening more and more, though.

L: That's right – the 'gig economy', they call it ... You know, freelance work, employing people on very short-term contracts, things like that ... I was reading about this cycling food delivery service app ... The technology means that the employer can monitor the workers almost at all times. One day the bosses tried to implement a new pay scale. The riders, of course, didn't want to earn less than the minimum wage, they didn't want their pay to be based only on the number of deliveries, so eventually they went on strike ... They didn't feel treated like employees at all.

B: I read that in some countries they're even thinking of linking teachers' pay to the students' test and examination results ...

L: Noooooo?

B: Yes!!! Can you imagine? Instead of education, you'd get exam preparation all year round!

L: All the important aspects of children's education would be ignored ...

B: Yes ... And in the meantime, so many chief executives are rewarded with huge bonuses, despite the fact that their individual performance is so hard to measure.

L: I think performance-based pay may be all right for very routine jobs, you know, when people repeat the same tasks all day long. However, just like you I believe that in most cases what employees need in order to get more motivated is recognition, they need to feel appreciated …

🔊 5.02

1 You work hard, we all know that, and you get a fair wage. However, perhaps a pay rise or a bonus of some sort would motivate you to work even harder ….

2 I simply do my best, I find satisfaction in what I do, and really, although not all my projects are very successful, I can't see how I could possibly work better or more.

3 Financial incentives are important, of course, but on the other hand, it would be a very sad world if we only worked to earn a better salary.

4 These days you hardly ever hear that word, do you? It's all about productivity, competition, things like that, although what we need most, in my opinion, is to be part of a group with common interests and objectives.

5 Yeah…It's happening more and more, though.

6 And in the meantime, so many chief executives are rewarded with huge bonuses, despite the fact that their individual performance is so hard to measure.

🔊 7.01

Speaker 1
I work for a manufacturing company, in the accounting division. Officially, the work day is from 8.45 to 5.15, but my colleagues and I almost always work until at least six, and often until seven. We occasionally leave on time on a Friday evening. Honestly, we aren't that busy, but the boss normally works until seven, and so we feel we should, too. This may sound crazy, but if I worked efficiently, I could probably finish my work at four o'clock every day. But we all want the manager to think we're busy and working hard, so we stay late at work on a daily basis. This is just working life where I live, and I don't think it will change.

Speaker 2
My work week has recently been cut from forty to thirty-five hours, but with no cut in pay, amazingly. A year ago, we started looking at efficiency. We measured the time we were spending on different tasks, and we discovered that we wasted many hours each week on meetings. We started to be very careful about who attended meetings and also worked very hard to make the meetings short. Now, meetings are usually about fifteen minutes at the

longest, and we have certain times in the day when everyone turns off email. We occasionally work a bit of overtime, but not often. And we almost always hit our targets ahead of time. The business is doing great, and everyone is happier doing more work in fewer hours.

Speaker 3
I'm a freelance business consultant – I run my own company, but it's just me. I normally work on contract for larger organisations, trying to help them solve problems they're having with their business. This means I don't spend much time in my own office – only a few days a month. I usually go to work at my clients' offices for a period of two to three weeks. I try to identify ways they could improve efficiency and reduce time waste – that's usually the problem – low productivity. I try to lead by example. When I'm working in-company, I always arrive on time at the start of the work day, I never skip lunch, and I leave the office on time at five o'clock on a daily basis. I love my work, but it's incredibly important to me to have my weekends and evenings free to do other things that I really enjoy.

Speaker 4
Last week, I went out every evening after work for a meal that was related to work. I almost never spend more than forty hours per week in the office, but I often spend five or six hours a night after work socializing with colleagues or entertaining clients. On the one hand, this can be enjoyable and relaxing, but on the other hand, it's exhausting. I can never completely relax when I'm with a client, because it's all about business.
I need to make sure that our clients feel completely happy with the work we're doing together. And when I'm with colleagues, it's usually either people I manage, or people who I report to, so I have to be careful with my behaviour in both situations! But this is the nature of the field I work in, and so I guess I'll carry on doing it.

1.1 Stress in compound nouns

🔊 P1.01

car loan
card payment
credit card debt
dress code
fund transfers
job application
pay structure
working atmosphere

company practices
customer support representative
minimum salary

1.2 Auxiliary verbs in the Future Continuous and Future Perfect Simple

🔊 P1.02

1 By the middle of the next century, workplace culture will have changed drastically.

2 We hope our employees care whether or not we'll be making a profit in the future as our success depends on it.

3 Within a few years, these new initiatives will have made a real difference.

4 My company just announced that next year they'll be changing the dress code to business casual.

5 There's a lot of discussion about what companies will be doing in the future to keep their employees motivated.

6 The Managing Board has announced that in order to retain young staff members, they'll have implemented a scheme for swifter promotions by the beginning of next year.

🔊 P1.03

1 By the middle of the next century, workplace culture will have changed drastically.

2 Within a few years, these new initiatives will have made a real difference.

3 The Managing Board has announced that in order to retain young staff members, they will have implemented a scheme for swifter promotions by the beginning of next year.

🔊 P1.04

It is expected that the market will have recovered by close of business today.
They'll be hoping for a new investor who'll have the experience to turn the company around.
By that time, I hope they will have accepted our bid.
It'll be some time before all the markets will have recovered.

2.1 Stressing key words in sentences

🔊 P2.01

1 a The mentor is there to act as a guide and offer support.
   b The mentor is there to act as a guide and offer support.

2 a Training and development is a critical function in a modern business.
   b Training and development is a critical function in a modern business.

3
  a Because the world is constantly changing, we all need <u>to learn to adapt</u>.
  b Because the <u>world is constantly changing</u>, we all need to learn to adapt.

2.4 Linking between words
🔊 P2.02

Facilitation in professional context is the art of leading discussions and meetings.

It is a set of skills which guides people to discuss openly and productively.

In practice, it means confirming the objective a discussion, helping people feel confident to express their ideas, helping people to listen to each other, ensuring all ideas are considered, and supporting people to come to the best decision.

Without effective facilitation, meetings can become a waste of time.

Most meetings have a facilitator but are often more effective if all the people at the meeting share responsibility and help facilitate the discussion.

3.3 The letter 't'
🔊 P3.01

1 **a** just a little issue
  b the cheapest option
  c confident and optimistic
  d invest in new technology
2 **a** the next full project meeting
  b we can't run a project like this
  c just like I predicted
  d just to see what's going on
3 **a** I'm sure that we can turn this around
  b but only if we act now
  c think about it
  d a lot of money
4 **a** not a bad result
  b under target
  c I'm going out there
  d quite constructive
5 **a** just try
  b you don't trust them
  c the next full project meeting
  d over budget a little

3.4 Strong and weak forms of *that*
🔊 P3.02

1 That wasn't what I meant.
2 Could you say that again?
3 Do that again, and you'll regret it!
4 Could you repeat that, please?
5 OK, so that means we won't be finished before 11 a.m.
6 That gives us the average revenue.

4.1 Stress in word-building
🔊 P4.01

1 convert
2 analyst
3 conversion   converted   disruptive disruptor   prediction   predictive
4 innovator   innovative   irritable irritated
5 anticipate
6 irritation
7 anticipated
8 analytical
9 anticipation

4.4 Stress in phrases
🔊 P4.02

1 Let's think about how to manage this.
2 How could you imagine this working?
3 Tell me about how this situation affects you.
4 What do you think of this?
5 I'll let you know if I'm struggling.
6 Think of some other options to present at the meeting.
7 Get some expert advice before making a decision.
8 Let's try and look at this in the morning.
9 Why don't we approach it from another perspective?
10 It's a great idea, but it's unsatisfactory.

5.2 Intonation and linking words
🔊 P5.01

1 On the one hand, employees have to work more hours, but on the other hand, they receive overtime pay or extra time off.
2 In spite of launching a new and innovative product line, they have lowered their profit expectations.
3 Even though no performance scheme will fit every occasion, the fuel-saving study does suggest an approach worth trying more broadly.
4 Although salaries were not increased for captains, the fact that the company was taking an interest in fuel saving, and acknowledging success, seemed to delight them.
5 Executives are often those who receive performance-related pay. Nevertheless, it is often difficult to evaluate how well they have performed.
6 Despite finding that rewards could lead to employee motivation, management decided to stop the rewards system completely.
7 On the one hand, we keep getting more and more work to do. On the other hand, we were told by management that we shouldn't work overtime.

8 Despite the fact that the targets were set in discussion with department heads, they are proving to be unrealistic in some areas.
9 In spite of the fact that several experiments had shown that it was less effective than other schemes, they continued to use performance-related pay.

5.3 Intonation when handling challenging feedback
🔊 P5.02

1 **a** Yes, but <u>you're</u> not seeing the big picture here. Most of the chat is work-related, <u>actually</u>.
  b Yes, but you're not <u>seeing</u> the big picture here. Most of the chat is <u>work</u>-related, actually.
2 **a** There's room for improvement, I agree, but we've talked about this <u>before</u>. <u>You</u> have to remember that we predicted this might happen.
  b There's room for improvement, I agree, but we've <u>talked</u> about this before. You have to remember that we predicted this <u>might</u> happen.
3 **a** Well, I'm not sure what you're saying is necessarily <u>accurate</u>. It's true that a few employees park there because it's more convenient, but 'full' <u>is</u> an exaggeration.
  b Well, <u>I'm</u> not sure what you're saying is necessarily accurate. It's true that a few employees park there because it's more convenient, but <u>'full'</u> is an exaggeration.

6.2 Contractions and weak forms in third conditionals
🔊 P6.01

1 **A:** If they'd donated even 1 percent of the money they'd made to local projects, it would have generated really good publicity for them.
  B: Really? Do you think 1 percent would have been enough?
2 **A:** Would you have taken the job if they'd offered it to you?
  B: Yes, I think I would have.
3 **A:** How else could we have reduced our costs?
  B: Well, it might have been a good idea to have more virtual meetings.
4 **A:** Did you consider how much we could have reduced our tax bill if we'd given some of our profits to charity?
  B: Yes, it would certainly have been quite a lot.
5 **A:** They could have cut their carbon emissions considerably if they'd had a policy in favour of sourcing materials locally.
  B: Yes, they certainly could've.

6 A: They wouldn't have had such problems with stakeholders if they hadn't been so secretive about their finances.
B: No, they certainly wouldn't've.

6.5 Chunking, pausing and stress when reading aloud
🔊 P6.02

We encourage all staff to participate in our programme, so you could become a community hero, too. We are currently establishing a project to turn neglected public spaces into useful community gardens where local residents can grow both vegetables and decorative plants. Therefore, if you are interested in gardening or just enjoy working outside, please contact Human Resources immediately.

We are going to run a competition next month so staff can suggest ideas for other projects we can be involved in.

7.2 Stress and intonation in adverbials and time expressions
🔊 P7.01

1 rarely   seldom
2 normally
3 any day
4 almost never   hardly ever
5 at the latest
6 on a daily basis

🔊 P7.02

1 Sometimes she works over lunch.
2 Normally I don't work on Fridays.
3 They almost never leave the office before 7 p.m.
4 Many of us sit at our computers all day.
5 From time to time she does administrative work.
6 Usually meetings last about three hours.
7 They put in many hours on a daily basis, but they rarely work at the weekend.
8 You can come by to see me any day.

7.4 Intonation when negotiating
🔊 P7.03

1 I know we're both on the same wavelength about their experience.
2 So what you're saying is you definitely won't go?
3 I understand your position, and reluctance, a bit more now.
4 This is a good thing that we can all learn from.
5 In other words, you don't want to send either of them?

🔊 P7.04

1 How would you feel if we put you in charge of the project?
2 In your opinion, it should take around a month of local support. Right?
3 We're going to have to go the extra mile to meet the deadline.
4 What that means exactly is that we need to make this a priority.
5 I think we can both agree that we need to develop new workflows.

🔊 P7.05

1 How would you feel if we put you in charge of the project?
2 In your opinion, it should take around a month of local support. Right?
3 We're going to have to go the extra mile to meet the deadline.
4 What that means exactly is that we need to make this a priority.
5 I think we can both agree that we need to develop new workflows.

8.2 /s/, /z/, /ʃ/, /tʃ/ and /dʒ/
🔊 P8.01

1 classes
2 application,   sure,   technician
3 necessary,   process
4 courageous,   graduating
5 questions
6 clause,   closed,   colleagues,   figures
7 administration,   special
8 once,   personal
9 touch

🔊 P8.02

1 shares
2 clause
3 advice
4 advise
5 passion
6 mortgage
7 subjects
8 colleagues
9 location
10 transition
11 courageous
12 technologies

8.4 Voice range
🔊 P8.03

Brainstorming generates ideas which other methods do not, due to the freedom it gives people to think creatively. There are no 'golden rules' as such, but these eight stages can definitely help you to have successful stages:
1 Define the goal or desired outcome and the amount of time available.

2 Start with a question or selection of questions.
3 Collect as many ideas as possible, without evaluating them or commenting other than to thank each person for their ideas.
4 Put all of the ideas somewhere everyone can see them, for example, on a board. Then you all decide, how to group the ideas.
5 Ask people to give more details about their ideas before evaluating any of them.
6 Only at this point should you start to discuss, evaluate and build on the ideas.
7 Always end with some clear decisions and action points. And finally,
8 Thank everyone for participating. Even if some individuals didn't come up with the final idea, their presence helped to create the atmosphere that led to the outcome.